A Poem Called Lost

A Poem Called Lost

Margaret Peacock

Forward Movement Publications
Cincinnati, Ohio

Forward Movement Publications
412 Sycamore Street
Cincinnati, Ohio 45202

For Brian Roksiewicz
1982-1997
With love, always, for allowing me
to be your big sister.

The Rev. Margaret Peacock
is a deacon working
in the small community of St. Ignace
located far north on the
Straits of Mackinac where
Lakes Huron and Michigan meet.

Contents

Introduction

I wanted to write about the people God speaks for, who are unable to speak for themselves. This book is a result of that effort. The autistic, the battered, the mentally ill—I have met and known them and have finally been impelled to tell their stories. The boy who cries all night in seclusion in a mental hospital, the man who walks from city to city with garbage bags instead of shoes on his feet, the homeless family from whose midst only one member—the dog—finds a home, the autistic woman who hurls her communion bread down the aisle and talks to the stained glass windows—these are real people who, refusing to be "lost," still maintain their innocence and sense of humor. I have known these people, loved them, despaired over them, and passed on, but one thing I could do for all of them was, through the medium of these stories, to bring them together in community—the community of a church called St. Jude's.

The Rev. Margaret Peacock

If I take the wings of the morning
and dwell in the uttermost parts of the sea,
Even there your hand will lead me
and your right hand hold me fast.

Psalm 139

Too long a sacrifice
Can make a stone of the heart.

William Butler Yeats
Easter 1916

St. Jude's

St. Jude's church on the corner of Coffee and Keeler streets, in a medium sized midwestern city, in a neighborhood more sad than scary in the daytime, (though far less reassuring after dark) is the oldest Episcopal church, with the smallest congregation, in that town. The congregation rarely equals twenty, and there are few, infrequent visitors on Sundays—the kind of guests who decide on Christmas, Easter, and personal anniversaries, to renew their acquaintance with church. Other visitors (like myself) sometimes wander accidentally through the unlocked double doors.

People new to St. Jude's are always surprised to find that the rector, Father Joseph, has a ten dollar bill framed and mounted on the wall in his office.

"Why, Father?" they ask, and if he believes that they sincerely want to know, he'll tell them the story.

Just as he told me . . .

Perhaps I'd better say that I never intended to become a member of St. Jude's. I discovered the church because I hopped off a crosstown bus at the wrong stop. I found myself in a place where people would, against all my expectations, throw out a lifeline to someone who was alone.

When I boarded the bus, that warm spring Thursday, after leaving my apartment, I had no destination in mind. I was going to ride the bus across the city as I'd done many times in the past eight months; not to arrive anywhere but to escape from the past by turning up somewhere else. Like a throwaway penny. Then I would return to the apartment, to more meals left uneaten, more nights without sleep.

I didn't care.

A stone had fallen and now my insides weighed like stone, and I rode the buses. To forget what could not be forgotten. And to run away from the person I used to be.

I was forty-three years old, a woman who had loved reading, mountain biking, gourmet cooking, writing poems and short stories whether anyone read them or not. Daniel read them, and some were written to him. I'd loved Daniel.

We'd been married for fifteen years, until the stone fell, ending Daniel's life and putting mine on hold. After eight months I didn't grieve so much anymore, but didn't bicycle or read or cook or write poetry anymore either. I rode the buses.

And tried to run away from the person who had once blithely scribbled down hopes and dreams.

I didn't know how to communicate, with myself or anyone else. The dreams had curled up and died, like a small wild animal waylaid by a vicious trap.

I was financially, if not emotionally, independent. I rode the buses during the day; returned at night to an apartment which was the opposite of home, and caught the bus again next morning.

There was a young man two seats ahead of me on the bus that particular Thursday afternoon. He was reading a magazine, which wouldn't have interested me except I could see it was a poetry magazine, and I read the title of one of the poems, embellished in huge black capital letters on the left hand page.

The poem was called "Lost." A picture on the next page showed a girl with long blond hair, standing by a low stone wall and holding an armful of flowers.

I was too far away to read anything else except that one word, "Lost."

I wasn't happy. I never am in situations like this. Call it an instinct to snoop, but I wanted to know more, a lot more. Something about the young man who was reading, and why he chose to stare and stare at that poem, without ever turning the page. I wanted to know who the author of the poem was, and to discover the title of the magazine, and to find out what the girl with the long hair intended to do with all those flowers.

I would not, of course, go up to a stranger and ask. Not on an inner-city bus.

But then it hit me. With a little burst of pain, as if I'd been pinched.

I was taking an interest in something. For the first time since the stone.

I was chewing my lip in frustration because of a poem. A poem called "Lost."

I rose and vacated that bus at its very next stop. And then took a good look around at the neighborhood.

Which, I thought, was not a good place to be seen loitering.

I hadn't been inside a church for years. Except for Dan's funeral. But I'd been taught in childhood that churches were places of safety. When I saw one down the block, I headed there.

I read my bus schedule. I saw it would be at least an hour before the next bus came. I decided to wait inside the church, if I could find anyone around to let me in.

I expected the front doors to be locked on a weekday afternoon. A church would lock up tight in a neighborhood like this one.

But the doors weren't fastened.

"No one bothers us," Father Joseph told me later. "Because of Hawley."

Later on I would be introduced to Hawley, but I didn't meet him on that first afternoon, which is probably a good thing. Hawley can make newcomers to St. Jude's a little nervous.

I pushed the doors, which were already standing ajar, (and which desperately needed a few new coats of red paint) and crept into the old, run-down building whose stories and people I would soon come to know so well.

St. Jude's is a very large church, built sometime toward the end of the last century, with a tiny congregation, many of whom will probably not live to the end of this century. The disparity in the size of the church and the size of the congregation isn't odd, not this day and age.

But what I saw when I stepped into the sanctuary, seemed unaccountably strange.

On age-weary grey concrete walls, between every one of the twelve large stained glass windows, most of which were cracked or defaced ("done before Hawley," Father

Joseph told me later) hung a vast and gaudy assortment of jigsaw puzzles. The five-hundred-to-one-thousand-piece variety of puzzles. They'd all had adhesive affixed to the back so that they couldn't be taken apart again. And there seemed to be at least a hundred of them fixed to the walls.

The jigsaw puzzles didn't prepare me for what I saw when I walked up the aisle toward the altar.

It was a very small altar for the size of the chancel. It was wooden, painted white, and removed from the wall. What made me rub my eyes was the presence of two very elderly men standing one on each side of the altar, and mumbling contentedly to themselves while they played checkers.

Without a checkerboard, because they had none.

The surface of the altar, bare of hangings, *was* the board. Or boards. For they had two games going on at once, one on each end of the altar.

Moving closer I could see that sixty-four squares had been carved into the wood on both ends, and painted black and white so that two boards were formed, with the center of the altar intact between them.

Two sets of hand-carved, oversized wooden checkers nestled snugly into the recessed squares, giving each end of the altar the look of a giant candy box, of white and chocolate confections.

The two old men continued playing, oblivious of me. I'd never seen anything like it, and I didn't know what to think.

This wasn't "church" as I remembered it from childhood.

St. Luke's, where I had spent most of my Sundays when growing up, would never have countenanced this effrontery.

"It startles most people, seeing Fred and Jerry playing checkers," said a voice behind me.

I jumped, startled not by Fred and Jerry but by hearing a man's voice, unexpectedly.

"They always play checkers in the afternoons. Except Mondays, when the youth group uses the boards to play chess."

I turned and found myself confronting a tall, Hispanic man in his early fifties. A man with the kindest and saddest dark brown eyes I'd ever seen.

He was wearing faded jeans and a torn sweatshirt, but I knew without asking that he was the priest. Some instinct left over from all those Sunday services at St. Luke's.

Maybe I was still thinking about that poem, which I hadn't been able to read. Maybe it was still having so much hurt left, eight months after the stone, or the shock of seeing those two old men, so gleefully playing checkers on an altar. Maybe I just hadn't eaten for too long a time.

Whatever the reasons, to my dismay, as I tried to find the words to explain my presence to the priest, my nose went stuffy and my throat choked up and I started to cry.

I fished a handkerchief from the pocket of my jeans and did the best I could to hide behind it.

The priest didn't seem to mind.

"I'm Joseph," he said, holding out a hand. "The rector here. But you came from the bus stop, didn't you?"

"Meg Cavenaugh." I pulled myself together long enough to accept his handshake. "How did you guess? About the bus, I mean."

"Some people come to us that way. Others—in other ways. You don't have any idea where you are, do you?"

I shook my head sadly. "No, I'm sorry." I hadn't a clue.

"This is St. Jude's Church."

"The patron of lost causes?" I did know that much.

Father Joseph smiled.

"Yes. But Sister Monica, who is our deacon, prefers to call him a patron of the 'gifted and talented.' So many of the people who come here have fallen on very hard times. But they're all unique. All extraordinary. Here at St. Jude's, we try to honor the 'gifted and talented' whom God sends us."

I hadn't heard anyone use the word "honor" for a very long time.

"Tell me about the altar."

He shrugged.

"Fred and Jerry live down the street. They've been playing checkers at home for years and years. When I came here four years ago, Fred's eyesight wasn't very good and Jerry was starting to have some memory problems. The two of them—along with our church organist—were the only members left from what used to be a fair-sized congregation. Fred came to me and said that they were having a lot of trouble playing, because he couldn't see the pieces on the board, and Jerry would get mad and throw the pieces, then wander away and forget to pick them up. They needed a large, flat surface and a way of making sure that the checkers could stay in place."

"And the altar was your idea?"

"Sister Monica—we sometimes call her 'Tall Monica,' to set her apart from 'Little Monica,' who plays the organ—had the idea first. She thought we should find a way to help Fred and Jerry."

"Didn't your congregation—your bishop—get awfully upset?"

He looked amused.

"Fred and Jerry were two-thirds of the congregation, and Little Monica, the other third, wasn't happy at first, but finally decided it was something she could live with. As for the bishop—"

His eyes twinkled.

"He talked me into coming here. And since we went to seminary together, he knows me very well, and has been very supportive of our 'unusual methods' here at St. Jude's."

He paused, and then continued,

"It wasn't a question of changing things, when I came here. Or even of reviving a dying church. St. Jude's, as it existed in the past, died a long, long time ago. What remained here was a pile of bricks and mortar, and a few very hungry church-rats down in the crypt."

He looked in the direction of Fred and Jerry.

"Little Monica is St. Jude's only altar guild member. When she covers the altar for Sunday, sometimes she leaves the checkers in their grooves and places the altar hangings on top. While I'm reading the service I often think about those pieces, lying so safely hidden, underneath . . ."

He sighed, and glanced at his watch.

"Are you in a hurry? Do you need to catch the next bus? I'd be happy to go on talking about St. Jude's, but I don't want to delay you if you have to go."

"I'm not in a hurry," I said, "and there isn't any place where I have to be. That's part of the problem."

He studied my face, which was still goose-pimply from crying.

"There's coffee in my office. We can talk there."

His office was a small and sparsely furnished room, which he said had been added to the sacristy as an afterthought years ago. I could still see flaking paint traces of the word "storage" on the door.

But a window in the room was open, and a warm spring breeze wafted through. Outside, in the middle of the parking lot, a single tall, slim maple tree had new leaves, and in a patch of garden at one end of the church courtyard there were red and white flowers.

He made two cups of coffee from a coffeemaker propped on top of a theology book and a volume of T.S. Eliot's poetry, on a rickety bookcase sagging against the rear wall.

The coffee, and also his silence, encouraged me to talk.

I told him how, and why, I'd stopped writing. I told him about Daniel, and about the stone.

Stone?

"It was a thirty-five-pound boulder. They must have carried it in a car, up onto the overpass. I'm sure whoever did this thought it was a wonderful prank. To drop a boulder off an overpass—" I swallowed hard. "And onto the roof of Daniel's car. He was coming home from work. Like he did every weekday—just coming home, after picking up a few groceries, on a Wednesday afternoon."

I felt the weight of the stone, heavy inside me again.

"It isn't the broken glass, or even the bloodstains left in the car after they peeled out Daniel's body, which still give me nightmares. It's the orange juice and the milk, spilled together all across the back seat. From two smashed cartons, milk and orange juice in one big puddle. And you know what? The dozen eggs he'd bought didn't even get broken. I took those home with me, sometime later. And I smashed every one of them against our bedroom walls. I cleaned it up, and after the funeral I sold the house. And I'm never going to be able to write again because of the stone. It killed all my stories when it killed Daniel."

The priest didn't argue, just listened. From somewhere, deep in the bowels of the church I believed I could hear a harmonica playing, and I wondered what sort of church I'd stumbled into, and if (as I often feared during long, sleepless nights) I was going (or already had gone) crazy.

Father Joseph was silent for a long while after I had finished. Then he sighed.

"I cannot promise you that the stories will come back to life. They may or may not, but even if you decide not to write, you need help to get rid of the stone."

He saw me looking at the ten dollar bill hanging on

the wall. I focused my attention on the bill so that I would not see any pity in his eyes.

There wasn't any pity in his voice as he continued.

"I didn't believe I'd escape from hell, either, until a very kind lady gave that to me."

I did look back at him, then, and he nodded in the direction of the money.

"She took the stone off my soul."

He went on to tell me about Dominique.

A Poem Called "Lost"

He sits and reads
a poem called "Lost"
while people haul themselves aboard
the bus
      and then get off.
I'd like to read
the words across
his shoulders
but
      I can't see anything, except
that one word, "Lost," *and then*
a picture of
a girl.
A girl with flowers:
      not looking lost.
I leave the bus
and he's still sitting—
detached from others
never turning the page—
      staring and staring
at a girl with flowers:
      reading, re-reading
a poem called "Lost".

Dominique

Father Joseph sets his coffee cup on the desk, swivels around in his rickety office chair, and rests his elbows on its cracked and faded, blue upholstered arms.

His voice is very quiet as he begins.

"It happened so long ago, and in such a different reality, that sometimes it seems like a dream . . .

"I was born in a very rural area, in a part of this country where there are a lot of immigrants, a lot of desperately poor people, a majority of people who don't speak English.

"I grew up in a small border town, which never had a census taker come there, and never made it onto a map, that I've ever heard tell. My mother was Hispanic, and when I was growing up in the 1950s, she worked as a cook at a restaurant which served burgers, mostly, but also some fancier items for those who could afford to pay. In a separate building next door, but owned by the same man, was our town's largest bar. I grew up thinking nothing of seeing drunks stagger down the street at all hours. We rented a tiny apartment within a quarter mile of the restaurant, and my mother was able to walk to and from work.

"My father was Italian, but he disappeared from our lives when I was only six months old. I wanted a father, and I used to tell my friends that he was a rich man, and invent stories about where he was, and what he was doing. I longed to see the ocean, and sometimes I imagined that my father had a mansion in some Hollywood movie type city, and a sailboat moored nearby, and when I was old enough he would come and take me away to live with him on the beach-front and go sailing."

He shrugs.

"In a world as poor as mine was, it helped to have dreams. Though my mother sometimes smacked me for not doing chores, and not 'keeping my face to reality.' I can hear her voice now. 'Joseph! When are you going to face reality? Stop daydreaming and take the garbage out.' But I always knew that I was missing something—that there was another reality I was hoping to find."

He looks around the office.

"My mother was not a church-goer. There was a Roman Catholic church in the town, but I never went inside it. I used to pass by its grounds, though, every time I went to meet my mother at the restaurant. There were always pigeons sitting on the old, crumbling grey roof. They would fly off as I approached. And I thought what a wonderful thing it must be, to fly into the sky like a dove . . .

"Sometimes I even tried to fly away, by flapping my arms.

"The restaurant was a bad place to work. My mother hated it there, but in a town like ours, where so many people were unemployed, she considered herself lucky to have work.

"'We have to eat,' she told me. 'Otherwise, I would take the scrap bucket and throw it at Diablo, as he throws it at me. And I would find a job that pays more money, so that I could buy myself a new dress, and you a bicycle. But it won't happen. Life doesn't work out like that, Joseph.'

"She was talking about the manager of the restaurant, a surly, mean-tempered little man named Diego, but whom all the staff called 'Diablo' behind his back. He was not an evil man, I think, just very angry and frustrated. The owner, who lived in northern California and only came back three or four times a year to see how his property was doing, took it out on Diego if the restaurant didn't make enough money. And Diego took out his anger on his two waitresses, and on the kitchen staff, of whom my mother was in charge.

"They fought constantly, my mother and Diego, though he never fired her. I think he always hoped that she would agree to sleep with him, even though he already had a wife and a mistress. My mother would rather have been dropped into a tank of red hot frying oil than go out with Diego. And yet she needed the wages he paid her. So they fought and insulted each other until it became a kind of game, a way of life which made it harder than ever, working in that place. And the other staff heard and copied them, and fought each other, but did not enjoy the same immunity from Diego as my mother."

Father Joseph shakes his head.

"I have seen that man lose his temper and throw fistfuls of food at his waitresses. I have seen him throw a garbage can full of food at my mother's head, miss her and hit the wall, and then the busboy had to clean it up, glass and grease and stinking scraps, off the floor and wall. It was a very, very bad place to work, that restaurant, and the food they sold was not even very good. My mother couldn't do all the work by herself and, as you can imagine, Diego had trouble keeping help. But in those days, in a town like ours, you didn't complain. You either kept the job, or quit and fervently prayed to find another."

He pours himself another cup of coffee.

"Most days of the year, children of employees were not allowed in the restaurant. When I was very small, my mother stayed home with me in the daytime and had a neighbor woman in to sit with me in the afternoon and at night, because she worked a ten-hour shift, from four in the afternoon until two in the morning, when the restaurant closed and only the bar remained open. Later on, from the time I was seven or eight, I stayed home alone at night until the restaurant closed, and then I would walk there at two a.m., cut through the alley, knock on the back door, and meet my mother. I would walk her safely home, and I was proud of being man enough to do this.

"When I was eight, Diego decided that I was old enough to start doing a few small jobs around the restaurant after school and at night. I was glad for the small amount of money that he paid me, glad to be able to spend more time with my mother, and I didn't even mind being bossed around by the busboy. What I didn't like was coming home with the smell of that place—the stink of grease and garbage and old stale food on my hands and in my hair.

"Once again, my mother tried to discourage me from dreaming.

"'What do you think, that you're going to grow up to become a rich man? Face reality, Joseph. You'll be working in a place like Diego's for the rest of your life. Only, pray God you work for someone with a better temper.'

"Somehow, I don't know how, I managed to keep my hopes alive.

"The summer I was nine, Diego hired a young woman to wash dishes in the kitchen. Her name was Dominique, and I doubt if she was more than twenty-three or twenty-four. She was not like anyone I had ever met. She was Caucasian, and had obviously been born in the United States, but no one knew where she came from, or what she was doing in our village. She didn't dress, act, or talk like the women I knew.

"She wasn't pretty—her hair was mousy brown and she was very pale and thin and wore oversized glasses which hung crookedly on her nose—but she was quiet and comforting to be around, and she had a wonderful, penetrating smile which made me want to grow up overnight, marry her, raise a family with her, follow her anywhere. She did her work silently and well, never raising her voice or talking back to anyone in the heat and screaming chaos which was that kitchen. But frequently, as she saw me struggling to carry out garbage cans which were twice my size, and pushing a broom around endlessly dirty corners of counter and floor, she would smile and nod encouragingly, as if to reassure me that I had a friend.

"'She must have done something shameful,' my mother said; 'Been thrown out by her family, or divorced by her husband—something very bad, to be alone, and working here.'

"But I didn't see how Dominique could ever be accused of being bad.

"My mother and Diego couldn't care less about her past, as long as she got her work done and didn't break too many cups or plates. And the children, many of them my friends, who hung around the back alley of the restaurant hoping for a little free food or the chance to do an errand and earn some money, liked her as much as I did. She worked from eleven in the morning till eight at night, and brought her own lunch and dinner—almost always a sandwich or a small metal thermos full of hot coffee or soup—rather than paying to have a meal served to her in the kitchen. Unless it was raining she ate outside, sitting on the back steps of the restaurant, where other employees joined her to eat, take their breaks, and smoke endless, cheap, unfiltered cigarettes.

"Dominique would share her lunch with any child who came around.

"'You shouldn't give food to those brats,' one of the two bad tempered, sour old spinsters who were our waitresses scolded. 'They'll never go away and leave us alone.'

"The other waitress, Juanita, who was as angular and hard-mouthed as her friend Maria was fat and pouty, nodded agreement.

"'These children—except for that one over there; he's my nephew—they would steal us all blind if we let them. You don't know this town. You don't know our ways here. In a few weeks you'll get fed up and then move on.

But we have to live with these brats coming by with their hands out.'

"Dominique said nothing, just smiled that same warm, slightly peculiar smile, which seemed to say that she knew something the rest of us didn't.

"'Do you know what I'm going to do, Joseph?' she asked me one evening, in late September.

"I rubbed my eyes sleepily, only half paying attention, because I was back in school again now, and it was hard to get enough sleep while going to school in the daytime and hanging around the restaurant waiting for little jobs to do at night.

"Besides, I wasn't supposed to be talking to Dominique or any of the other employees unless my mother or Diego permitted it.

"But she stood there beside the cheap, inadequate little dishwashing machine and the garbage cans full to overflowing with stale food; she stood there with sweat running down her face and making limp twisted rags of her long hair, and she flashed me that wonderful smile.

"'I am going to take twenty dollars of my pay, and eat in the private dining room of this restaurant on Christmas Eve.'

"'What?' I was astonished.

"Employees didn't eat in the dining room of the restaurant. Not that it wasn't allowed—Diego was glad to take money wherever it came from—but why would any of us want to eat in a place that had all the ambience of a battlefield kitchen in the Second World War?

"And the private dining room—only the very few, very pampered or most important customers whom the owner knew were invited to eat in there. The owner and his family when they came, or local government officials whom Diego needed to bribe to stay in business.

"How did a kitchen maid, a pot scrubber, a plate scraper, think she was going to be allowed in the private dining room?

"It became a joke when she told the other employees. The two waitresses, Maria and Juanita, almost doubled over laughing.

"I know now that they were jealous of Dominique; jealous of her youth and her competence and the uncomplaining way in which she did her job; of her ability to make friends with those they had deemed untouchable, and above all of the fact that nothing they said or did was able to upset her. Not insults or rude teasing or even the occasional shove in the ribs as she walked into the dining room to give them back a load of cups or plates.

"'Why don't they leave her alone?' I asked my mother.

"'Hush. There are some things you don't understand yet,' she replied in a voice which warned me to drop the subject.

"But she, too, wondered about Dominique's talk of eating in the private dining room on Christmas Eve.

"'Perhaps Diego has yelled at her so often,' my mother said, 'that she's gone a little crazy.' Though my mother fussed and shouted at the dishwashers and the busboy just as often, when she did so herself, she believed it was in a good cause.

"She did not believe, for a moment, that Dominique was serious, only touched in the head.

"But all that fall, Dominique kept children on the back

steps entertained, by telling us what items on the menu she hoped to order, and how hard she was working to save the money. In those days twenty dollars was a lot of money for someone in her circumstances to contemplate spending on just one dinner. She couldn't spend that much at our restaurant, anyway, not even if she ordered the best dessert and a bottle of wine. Five dollars would buy her anything on the menu; none of us could understand why she talked about saving twenty.

"'Just trying to rub our noses in it,' said Juanita, whose disposition was so nasty that she never received very much in the way of tips.

"But I admired Dominique for her quiet effrontery in insisting that an impossible dream was possible.

"And I loved the fact that she didn't become angry with me, even when she caught me peeking into her backpack.

"She carried a burlap and canvas satchel everywhere she went. It had leather shoulder straps on it. I had never seen any woman carrying a bag like that around for her personal things. I thought perhaps the pack held a clue to her identity, and decided to risk finding out, for I desperately wanted to know who she was. But when I sneaked into the area where employees always left their possessions, and stuck my face into Dominique's satchel for examination one afternoon, I found nothing in it more exciting than an apple left over from her lunch.

"'Joseph.' I jumped, and raised my arm to ward off the blow I was sure was coming, as she walked in and caught me invading her property. 'Joseph. You know what you've just done is wrong, don't you?'

"I nodded; tears starting to run down my face. I didn't care if I was punished, as long as she would eventually forgive me. This was the one person in the world I didn't want angry with me.

"'Next time, ask, if you want to see what's in my bag. I'll be happy to open it for you.' And she gave me the apple.

"'Who are you? Really?' I dared to ask. I was so frightened that I whispered, but my curiosity forced me to ask.

"'A friend,' she whispered back.

"And that was as much about her personal life as I ever knew.

"Diego, fortunately, knew nothing about Dominique's grand plan, for he thought his time too valuable to spend listening to employee gossip, and even the waitresses never spoke to him willingly. Maria and Juanita disliked my mother and were envious of Dominique, but they loathed Diego for his crudeness and brutality, and would never tell tales to him about what they considered was only a dishwasher's boasting.

"They, themselves, did not want to look silly.

"Christmas Eve approached, and everyone waited anxiously, as we always did, for the only two days of the year when Diego was away from the restaurant. He always took his wife on a holiday—somewhere nice, in order to atone for his affairs all year long. On Christmas Eve my mother was always left in charge of the restaurant. We didn't begin our holiday until half past eleven in the evening, when the doors could be locked, the restaurant closed for the whole of Christmas day, and Maria and Juanita would hurry off for midnight mass.

"What my mother and I didn't know was that the two waitresses were planning to carry out a cruel prank on Dominique, who was still insisting that she would eat in the private dining room.

"They had decided to let her do what she wanted, once Diego was out of the way. They knew that my mother, who broke Diego's rules herself in a flagrant way every Christmas Eve, and dared them ever to say anything about it, would not interfere with their activities in the dining room. They would let Dominique eat in the private room, give her splendid service, and let her order whatever she wanted from the menu.

"And then, when she had eaten her food and paid for her meal—and there was no way that she could spend more than five or six dollars, even if she ate the most expensive meal in the house—then, they would refuse to give her back her change.

"They would pretend that they didn't know what she was talking about. That there was no change left in the till. That a dinner in the private dining room on Christmas Eve was triple the normal price. Whatever. They would break her legendary calm and make her so angry that she would go away, find a different job and leave them overjoyed that the victory which they coveted, had been won.

"Christmas Eve began as it often did, that far south, all warm and sunny. Since it was a school holiday, I accompanied my mother to work in the morning. With Diego away she would work a double shift to handle all the displaced customers who had no family, the divorced and single men, and people with relatives in town who were looking for a holiday meal but didn't feel like cooking it at home.

"Dominique had the day off, and the part time, relief dishwasher and the assistant cook were coming in to help out.

"As so many times before, walking past the Catholic church and watching the flock of white and grey pigeons on the roof, I wondered what people did inside that building, and what you had to do to get on the right side of this Jesus whose birthday we were about to celebrate tomorrow.

"In the world as I knew it up until that day, there were only strong people and weak people—people who survived and those who could not. I didn't know life could be lived any other way.

"The day dragged on into the evening, and as closing time approached and Dominique had not appeared, I began to think she had gotten scared and after so much talking had backed out of her decision and let us all down. I felt sad.

"And then, at ten o'clock, just when Maria and Juanita were hoping no further customers would show up, so that they could begin cleaning early and make their escape, Dominique walked into the dining room.

"She wore a plain, but pretty blue and white cotton dress, and she held a wallet open to show a twenty dollar bill. Juanita and Maria acted as if nothing were unusual. They wished her a merry Christmas, chatted with her, and led her through the main dining room, past the half dozen customers who were still sipping their wine and chewing their food, and unlocked the door to the small side room which had not been used since the owner ate there, three months previously.

"'She's ordered the chicken with walnuts,' the busboy whispered, a few minutes later. 'And a glass of white wine.'

"My mother pressed her lips together, half admiringly and half in wonder. 'Who is she, to think she can walk in so late, and place an order?' But she didn't sound angry. And then she nodded quietly at me, to go ahead and unlock the restaurant's back door.

"Diego never knew, for even the waitresses would not tell him, but on Christmas Eve she allowed children—both the children of employees, and the street urchins who waited in the alley hoping for a handout—to come into the back hallway where Rodrigo, the handyman and janitor, kept an eye on them and made sure that they behaved themselves and didn't steal anything.

"This was my mother's way of helping any employee who could not find a baby-sitter on Christmas Eve. It was also her way of getting even with Diego, for all the abuse suffered during the year.

"She would let employees who could keep their children quiet and out of trouble bring them in when they arrived to start their shift. The street children could come in, if they behaved themselves, when the door was unlocked as soon as the restaurant traffic slowed down.

"I remember what it was like, sitting with so many of my friends, crowded into that smelly little narrow hallway on Christmas Eve, seeing the eager, desperate anticipation on their faces, and waiting for the moment when church tower bells would chime half past eleven, the waitresses would hasten late-sitting customers out of the dining room, the dishwasher and my mother would hurry through their last-minute cleanup, and then my mother would come out with bags of food in a cardboard box, to give to each waiting child.

"It was always like this on Christmas Eve. And the only thing different about Christmas day was that we could sleep very late, I could open the few small presents my mother had managed to buy, and we always had plenty to eat for Christmas dinner. Because my mother made sure that I took a bag home, too.

"Christmas was never that much different from any other day. But this Christmas Eve was different, because Dominique was eating in the private dining room. 'She's sitting in the owner's wife's chair,' George, the busboy whispered.

"My friend Antonio was one of the children who fidgeted and squirmed in the back hallway. Only eight, a year younger than me, he suffered from rickets and bad teeth caused by malnutrition. He was not a healthy or handsome child. I kept him entertained in between running back and forth to help my mother by telling him stories of what must be going on in the dining room.

"'Do you think she's smacking her lips, over the food?' I asked. 'My mother put extra walnuts on the chicken, you know.'

"'I wish I had twenty dollars to spend on dinner,' Antonio said, enviously.

"Dominique had chicken with walnuts, green beans, mashed potatoes, and a huge piece of chocolate cake for dessert. George reported every detail of this glorious meal.

"'You should see Juanita's face. She hates waiting on Dominique,' he said gleefully. He had often been the target of a whack from Juanita's thin, hard hand.

"'I never thought I would see such a day. The dishwasher eating in the private dining room,' my mother sighed.

"George came running in, very excited. 'Dominique is in the main dining room! Making a scene! She went to pay her bill, and Maria wouldn't hand over her change! They are telling her that they won't give her the fourteen dollars she has coming back! She says if they don't give her the change, she'll tell the rest of the customers she's been robbed.'

"'Those fools!' my mother snapped. 'If she makes a scene, someone will tell Diego. And we'll all be in trouble.' She tore her apron off, and ran through the wooden double doors leading to the dining room.

"I peeked through the doors, beyond which I was not allowed to venture. Dominique was a pale thin fury confronting Maria and Juanita. 'You will let me have my change, and an apology, or I will start screaming so loudly, that people who are hanging their Christmas stockings in the next town will hear me,' she said, with a wrath of which I'd never thought her capable.

"My mother joined the fray, but Juanita and Maria were already backing down. 'It was only a joke,' they protested sullenly. 'Sorry.'

"'Give her what she's owed. And don't ever do anything like this again, when I'm in charge. Do you want us all to lose our jobs?'

Then she turned on Dominique. 'Look at the trouble you've caused. By not knowing your place. You have no right to ask for special favors. To act as if you're better than the rest of us.'

Dominique had recovered her composure. 'I have the right to be treated with respect.' She paused, and then a note of deliberation entered her voice. 'And so do you, and so does Joseph. Do you hear what I'm saying? As well as anyone else who ever has to work in a place like this.'

"Maria shoved a fistful of one dollar bills at Dominique. 'Here. Fourteen dollars in ones. Take the money, and go home. Wherever it is that you live.'

"Dominique stood and looked at her for a long moment. 'Merry Christmas,' she said finally. And she left the dining room and walked back through the kitchen. My mother stayed to give the two waitresses an additional piece of her mind.

"Dominique started toward the back door, still clutching her fistful of dollars. And then she stopped, as she almost stumbled headlong over Antonio, who had fallen asleep in the middle of the floor, his body in the corridor, his head sticking out across the threshold of the kitchen door.

"'What—?' she exclaimed, as she was suddenly confronted by the hungry, staring, and all too old eyes of nineteen children.

"'It's just the street children,' Rodrigo the janitor told her. 'Come to get their Christmas handout.'

"The assistant cook, a slim girl of eighteen, came into

the hall to see what was going on. The two-year-old asleep on a pile of potato sacks was her son Carlos.

"The relief dishwasher stuck his head through the door. He was in his mid-twenties. Two of the children, ages five and seven, belonged to him.

"Most of the children had met Dominique before, shared lunch with her, exchanged a few private words of comfort or humor. Now they flocked around her. 'Merry Christmas,' she whispered.

"Before any of us knew what was happening she was handing each child a one dollar bill from the wad in her hand.

"And she gave each child a hug or a pat on the head or got down on her knees with the littlest ones and looked into their eyes, and said simply. 'Merry Christmas.' Or, 'Bless you.'

"I crept into the hallway, and huddled up next to the wall. I didn't understand what was happening, but I felt as if something miraculous was taking place. My friends were laughing, crying, trying to follow Dominique as she moved from child to child, not wanting to be separated from the warmth and love and safety generated by that wonderful smile, by the voice saying, 'bless you.' Everyone received a dollar. George the busboy, who had just come into the hall; the assistant cook, and Rodrigo. My friend Antonio came stumbling over on his malformed legs, and she held him tight in her arms for a long, long moment before releasing him, blessing him, and handing him his dollar.

"There were more than twenty people, children and adults in the hall, and she ran out of the dollars clenched in her fist. I saw her run out; and yet somehow as if by magic, from her backpack and her wallet, she managed to bring out even more one dollar bills. She worked her way round to each child, each adult in the hall.

"Except me.

"And then she saw me crouching against the wall. She got down on her knees. 'Joseph. Do you know who I am?' I shook my head. I was, for some reason, suddenly frightened. And for the second time, encountering her unexpectedly, ready to cry.

"'Someday, you will know who I am.' She looked at me very intently. 'When people tell you that you have to be like all the others, that's wrong. Like going through my backpack was wrong. You must believe me, when I tell you that it really is all right to be yourself.'

"I nodded, trying to understand what she was talking about.

"'What do you want most in the world, Joseph?' I blurted out, without thinking, my most familiar fantasy. 'I want to go sailing with my father. On his big boat.'

"She smiled then, and I knew that she knew that I had no father, and I really did start to cry, huge tears that dripped and dripped down my face. She reached out and put a hand on my head. 'You will find your father someday, but not the one you expect,' she whispered softly. 'Remember this: the reason that you hurt more than other people, the reason you want to fly away like the wild birds—' She saw my startled look, and nodded, 'Yes, I know about how you watch the pigeons, and run down the street flapping your arms as if you could be one of them—I know all about you, Joseph and the reason you suffer more is because you have more to give. Remember that, and never turn anyone down. Bless you, for I have to go now.'

"She fumbled in her backpack, and produced a ten dollar bill. 'Pass this on to others, as you can.'

"No one had ever given me that much money without making me work very hard for it. I stared and stared at the ten dollar bill in my hands.

"She smiled that wonderful smile at me one last time, and then, straightening the glasses which had once more gone crooked on the end of her nose, she backed up, stood up, still looking at me, and said firmly, 'Never forget.'

"Antonio, who had dropped down to sit by my side, echoed her words. 'Never forget.'

"George the busboy mouthed the phrase. 'Never forget. Never forget.'

"Suddenly more than twenty adults and children were whispering, fiercely and in unison, while Dominique stood and walked to the back door. 'Never forget! Never forget! Never forget!'

"This outburst, born of all our longings, was perhaps the most remarkable thing about that Christmas Eve. 'Never forget! Never forget! Never forget!' It went on for several seconds, until my mother, having finished tongue-lashing Juanita and Maria, came running back to see what was happening. Dominique was gone, and the older children were babbling, while most of the younger children were still crying.

"'What on earth—!' my mother exclaimed, and turned to me for an explanation. But I had hidden my ten dollar bill by that time, and in all the confused welter of explanations, recrimination, excuses and apologies which followed, she never remembered to ask me if I had also received any money, and I never turned it over to her, though I was supposed to give her half of any money in my pockets at the end of the day for my clothing and school books.

"Dominique disappeared and I grieved for a long time, but my life went on. My friend Antonio died of pneumonia before Christmas Eve, the following year. My mother quit the restaurant, and found a better job as a sales clerk in a store, where she could be home with me at night, and where she was good at her job and was always treated with great respect.

"Diego's wife divorced him, and his mistress ran away with somebody else. Without my mother to hold things together the restaurant went out of business. I still stared at the pigeons on the roof of the Catholic church, but I was growing up, and I no longer flapped my arms like bird wings, up and down.

"Maria and Juanita managed to find, believe it or not, even at their ages of sixty and sixty-three, men unfortunate enough to marry them.

"I did very well in school; I won scholarships; I worked my way out of that town and went to college and then to seminary. And I never spent the ten dollar bill. I wanted to often enough; I needed to when times were very hard. But I also needed to keep it, to remember what Dominique said. About not giving up on myself. And passing gifts I received on to others."

Father Joseph's unfinished coffee has gone cold, and he pushes it away, across the desk.

"Dominique taught me something about God and human beings; something that isn't inside my theology books. I'm trying to use what she taught me, here at St. Jude's."

He hesitates.

"I still don't know who she really was. She told me I would understand someday, but I'm still not sure . . ."

He frowns for a moment.

"Jesus was a carpenter's adopted son. Perhaps an angel can be a dishwasher, or the other way round. I know I never, never laugh at people who tell me they believe in angels, and claim with such great excitement that they have seen one."

A Blessing

(Based on The Beatitudes)

Blessed are you;
Upheld are you;
Strengthened are you;
Set free are you—
Nourished are you;
Empowered are you;
Cherished are you;
Believed in are you—
Welcomed are you;
My loved-ones are you—
My loved-ones are you.

An Affirmation

Hear our prayers, Lord.

For strangers we meet
who have no home or hope or family;
For children we read of
sent from home against their will;
For children who run away
afraid of their families;
and others who cannot run
but are still in peril;

Strengthen their courage, O Lord;
and cause us to love them enough
that through loving they will have a home
someday.

For impoverished people
who survive and form communities
above and below the level of the street;
For those who are not aided by community
and yet survive still;
in prison or mental-health homes, hospital wards;
tenement housing or elder-care centers or
behind locked doors;

Show them that freedom still exists
through your infinite love;
Help us to give them that freedom
through dignity and love.

For those who feel
they are less human; those
who rage and threaten, harm themselves;
are different or crazy; those
who spit and curse
or weep, sitting on the street;
those who frighten the fully-human
with apathy and silence;

Break through that silence, Lord;
And remind us that these people, too,
are human—
have names
are our brothers and sisters, and you ask us
to be advocates for them;
to speak for them, to them
as if we were talking to you.

For those who have so little—
those who have nothing or never had
much to go on, to work with, to hold onto;
to call their own;
For those who once thought they were rich
but have lost all they valued;

Renew their trust, and comfort them;
Teaching us to love as we have always been
your loved-ones;
through you and in you and with you and for you;
Holding out a hand to this world.

Amen

Sister Monica

Sister Monica places an alarm clock on Father Joseph's desk. It's a new electronic model, battery operated, with lights that flash on and off and buttons which beep when pressed.

It looks like a U.F.O.

Father Joseph presses a button, and the clock chants the time at him.

"It's loud enough!" he protests. "What's this for, Packrat?"

Sister Monica laughs.

She is small and stocky, ebony complexioned with a close cropped thatch of grey hair, small pieces of which escape in disarray around her forehead, because she trims her hair herself. She is seventy-three but will admit to sixty-something, and the youth group has nicknamed her Tall Monica to distinguish her from Little Monica, who plays the organ and is actually three inches taller.

But Father Joseph calls her Packrat because of her vast collection of lost, donated, low-cost and discarded items which are filling a storeroom in the basement.

"The clock is to remind you when it's time to quit working and go home to bed," Sister Monica says.

"I don't need reminding," Father Joseph argues.

"Oh, yes you do."

"Home" isn't far away. The diocese has remodeled a

wing of the church which used to be the Sunday school annex, and converted it into an apartment for St. Jude's priest. The old rectory, a block away, is uninhabitable and scheduled to be torn down.

"You should talk," the priest continues, shaking his head. "How late did you stay here last night, taking inventory? And why didn't you ask me to help you with the paperwork, so that you could go home before midnight and get to bed?"

"I didn't want to bother you," Sister Monica says. "But I admit I almost fell asleep counting cans of Similac." She glances down at her arm, which has no wristwatch on it. "And I broke my watch again. Banged it on the door coming out of the basement."

"You and your one-dollar watches." Father Joseph makes the alarm clock beep and beep again.

"Why don't you buy a watch that won't fall off your wrist when you're crossing the street? Here, you need this alarm clock more than I do; why don't you take it?"

"I already have one," she confesses. "Yesterday I picked up six of these clocks at a rummage sale. Someone who needs a clock and can't afford one, will be glad to get one of them."

"Someone who has absolutely no desire to sleep late in the morning," Father Joseph says.

They are co-conspirators and close friends. Sister Monica lives with three other Episcopal nuns in a small, run-down building in a neighborhood even more poverty stricken than this one. She asked to be assigned to St. Jude's when she heard it was being re-opened, after having no minister (or congregation) for almost three years.

"St. Jude's has been a change for me," she says. "Easier, in some ways—I don't feel quite so desperate, working here. Not that this neighborhood doesn't have problems—we've got crime, drugs, prostitution and homelessness here, too. But the people living here haven't given up yet." She shrugs. "I've been a nurse for fifty years, a nun for forty-five years, and a deacon for fifteen. For most of my life, overseas and at home, I've been living in a war zone. I've counted up so many losses that now I think it's all right to spend the rest of my life 'finding' things for other people. Father Joseph is right; I am a scavenger. Of Similac and souls, but I can't list 'souls' on my inventory."

She sighs.

"I wake up in the night, and I tell myself I'm a thief. God's thief. Oh, not that I ever actually steal anything. But if there's something you don't need or don't want, then I'll be there with my truck, ready to take it away from you. I don't mind borrowing and begging, for people who have so little, from people who don't appreciate what they have."

Accompanied by Hawley, who is another friend and her vigilant shadow, Sister Monica drives her battered blue pick-up around the neighborhood in search of everything from gossip to good used furniture and people who need help. She will talk about those experiences which end on a light note—the man who traded a used refrigerator for a set of the Harvard Classics, or an individual who called her trying to find a home for his mother's fifteen cats. (Tall Monica placed them all.) She says almost nothing about the darker and more dangerous situations which she has encountered. But I have seen her talk an angry addict into putting down his knife, and submit to being arrested without violence. On the same afternoon, she buried the limp corpse of a stray cat in the garden off the courtyard of St. Jude's, and cried while she covered the grave with soft, wet earth.

Her storeroom in the basement contains not only the baby formula, but blankets and bedding, new and used clothing, toys, books, games, shelf after shelf of rummage sale items including kitchenware and small appliances, and box after box of canned food.

"A department store had a sale on umbrellas last week," Sister Monica says. "Don't worry, I'll find someone who can use them. I don't know about the box of 1980 presidential campaign stickers, though. For both parties. There's probably a market for collectors, but it's going to take some work on my part."

She loves opera and football, gardening and long walks in the rain. She regularly wears, loses, and is forced to replace the kind of cheap, perishable plastic watches which children own, and because these run so erratically she has never been known to arrive anywhere on time. This doesn't bother her. She is late, she explains, "on behalf of other people."

The more unorthodox a project seems, the better she likes it.

The checkerboards carved into both ends of St. Jude's altar were her idea, as were the jigsaw puzzles which now hang between the stained glass windows.

"We were trying to coax a few of the children who live near here into meeting at the church once or twice a week," she explains. "They needed an alternative to the street, but it had to be 'cool.' And then I thought about how much I liked solving puzzles when I was growing up. I had a case of brand new jigsaw puzzles in the storeroom. I don't think any of these children had ever seen a puzzle without half the pieces missing. We told any who were interested, that if they could put together one hundred jigsaw puzzles having five hundred pieces or more, in the months from Advent through Easter, we would put adhesive on the backs of all the puzzles and hang them in the sanctuary where everyone in the church could see them. And then Father Joseph decided that it might be a way to raise some money for improvements in the neighborhood. The parents of some of our children have been trying for years to get enough funds to finish building a playground. Father Joseph talked the diocese into pledging one hundred dollars for every puzzle the children actually completed. I don't think anyone believed our kids could do it, but when we dared the children to try, they threw themselves into the effort. They began coming in almost every evening during Lent. And you can see the results upstairs. We raised ten thousand dollars, the kids are still holding meetings here twice a week, the playground has been finished, and in addition to Jesus, Mary and Joseph on all the walls, we now have fjords, daffodils, alien spaceships and Bengal tigers. The idea might not work for other churches, but it made a big difference here. Our children have grown. And so has the congregation . . ." She pauses ". . . in imagination, and also in size. Sometimes we have as many as twenty people attending a Sunday service. That's a big change from four years ago, when the only people who stuck their heads in the door were Little Monica and Fred and Jerry."

We are standing in the storeroom. We are hot, dusty, and tired, for it is a warm June day and we have just finished the monthly inventory. Sister Monica, who never arrives anywhere on time, is nonetheless a strict and accurate record-keeper.

She wipes her face, and collapses into a deck chair in the corner of the room.

"Done. For another month," she sighs.

I drop into a second chair, beside hers. I pluck a cobweb from behind my left ear. I have been chasing dirt, dust and spiders off the walls and ceiling with a feather-duster and a broom for the past half hour.

Sister Monica is equally disheveled. But the bright orange scarf she wears around her neck seems clean and unmarked.

Whenever I see her she is invariably wearing something orange. A scarf or a belt which looks as if it came from Disneyland, or a handkerchief peeking out of her coat pocket. And sometimes on cold winter days, she shows up wearing a thick, astonishingly gaudy pair of woolen, hand-knit, orange and grey socks. Bulky enough to fill every crevice of the hiking boots she tromps through the snow with in the wintertime. And bright enough, as Father Joseph says, "to light her feet on fire, if the socks don't keep them warm enough otherwise."

He adds, "I never ask her where she found those

socks or who gave them to her. There are things it's safer not to know."

But now, as we sit among the canned goods and the umbrellas, the cases of Similac and boxes of Depends undergarments, the electronic alarm clocks in their rummage sale bags and the rows and double rows of old shoes, I ask her, not about the socks or the handkerchief or the belt, but about orange.

"It was the color of a child's old bathrobe," she begins.

One Dollar, Six Cent Watches

I've lost so many
one dollar, six cent watches (tax, you know)
in places God never invented.
One flew off my wrist
out the passenger window of a Volvo,
seventy miles an hour driving through Ohio.
Another wristwatch fell from
a Staten Island ferry—
and one remained in a rest room in some
small burger-palace in western North Carolina.

I don't pretend to be as careful of time as people who make their
living demanding,
other people arrive on time.

I don't get a thrill out of seconds
lighting up in the dark, either.
No, as imprecise as it sounds—
I'll keep on throwing
dollar-six-cent watches around.

For I guess I don't care very much about being on time—
As long as I get there
it's fine.

A Woman in Orange

"I was working as a nurse in a small mission hospital in Africa," Sister Monica says. "The name of the country doesn't matter. It was a long, long time ago. The idea of entering a religious order hadn't crossed my mind, but when I had finished my nursing degree I decided to take part in a program, sponsored by my university, which would send me overseas. I was young and idealistic, and I wanted very much to go to Africa. To do my share of good in this world, though I knew I was entering a difficult situation. What I didn't expect was the chaos which would overwhelm the hospital, only a few weeks after I had arrived there."

She shakes her head.

"The hospital was located in an area which had been drought-stricken for almost three years. The crops had failed again that year and people were suffering terribly from disease and malnutrition. In addition, a war was threatening to break out between several of the local tribes. I remember how frightened I was when I tried to go to sleep at night and could hear gunfire not so far away through the darkness. We were way, way out in the bush and in contact with the nearest town only by radio. It was difficult to have supplies shipped in to us, because truck convoys were frequently ambushed, and airlifts were difficult to arrange. Bandages, food and medicines were always in short supply, and we used all our supplies as sparingly as possible.

"From the time I arrived at the hospital I think I knew, but didn't want to admit, that I had made a mistake in coming there. I tried to do my job without complaining, but I was very frightened and inexperienced, as were all the other junior nurses—six of us embarked on training together. Three of us were sent by the same university; the other three were nuns belonging to the order which—though I did not know it yet—I would one day join.

"The head nurse was not a nun, but a coordinator of our overseas program who had lived and worked in many different African countries. She was in her late forties, a good administrator and skilled nurse, but not sympathetic when it came to overseeing her staff. She was quick to point out mistakes but seldom praised the three of us who looked to her for orders. The nuns who worked side by side with us had an easier time, for they were directed and supervised by a member of their order, who acted as liaison and peacemaker between them and the head nurse, Ursula.

"I had no such person to buffer me, and I was in conflict with Ursula from the time I reached the hospital until the time, two months later, when I fell ill.

"I know now that my own attitude caused a great deal of the friction which made our work so difficult. I had a short, sharp temper, and tended to snap back at people who criticized me. I was proud and considered myself a good nurse, and hadn't yet learned, as I would do very painfully in the years to come, that pride is the worst of seven sins.

"Ursula was determined not to coddle her staff. Perhaps she was trying to teach us a lesson how tough we had to learn to be in order to survive in a harsh land. But it was terribly difficult to work under someone who never smiled, never gave any words of encouragement. She saved all her kindness for the patients, with whom she never seemed angry or in a hurry. But for me it was always, 'This patient hasn't had her bed changed, Laura-Jean.' (That was my name, before I entered the order.) 'That bed should have been stripped down before you went running off to eat your dinner. I expect you to think about the patient's needs before you take care of your own. And if you can't move faster than that when I call you, maybe you'd be better off working at some other hospital.'

"It seems silly now, but I used to stick my tongue out at Ursula when she wasn't looking.

"I had one friend at the hospital, though. The youngest nun assigned there was twenty-four, my own age, and her name was Sister Miriam. She had a sense of humor which could banish my rebelliousness and anxiety even in that lonely place. She made fun of Ursula when no one else was around puffing out her cheeks and stamping her foot and giving orders in a bossy, impatient voice. 'Don't tell me it isn't your fault, Laura-Jean,' she would tease. 'Bring a bucket of water and scrub the floor. And haven't you given that patient with the cough her sponge bath yet? She was supposed to be given a bath, this morning. What? What excuse are you making now? You say the patient in that bed died this morning? Well, that isn't a good reason, Laura-Jean. You should have anticipated that, and bathed her yesterday.'

"Her laughter kept me sane. It was the only thing which helped me to survive two awful months. And then the war which had been threatening to break out exploded in a series of attacks and ambushes, as one tribe turned its fury on all the others. Entire villages were wiped out overnight and our hospital was suddenly swamped with refugees. We began treating gunshot and shrapnel wounds; the two doctors on our staff dressed burns and performed amputations.

"I was terrified as the war seemed to move in our direction. The doctors worked all hours of the day and night trying to keep pace with the sick and injured, even though there was so little morphine or ether left that they were forced to perform some minor operations without painkiller or anesthetic. We were almost out of penicillin and other antibiotics by the end of the second week of fighting, and had learned that there was no hope of a supply convoy reaching us. If supplies could not be air-lifted in we might have to evacuate, if the government would send troops to get us out. Until a decision was made, we were on our own. And in the meantime, as the fighting became worse, dead and dying people lined the corridors of the hospital, side by side with family members who crowded in anywhere they could, seeking food and shelter, or camped outdoors in the compound.

"We tried to maintain order, and to keep the one small operating room and the living space occupied by each patient as clean as possible. But it seemed to me that blood was everywhere, and that it was the only bright color in a place where black, brown, and white faces alike had taken on the ashen, death-hued complexion of desperation.

"There was nothing except pain on people's faces—pain which I could see and hear and smell—pain and terror accompanied by the bright, red blood and the sickly vile yellow of jaundice and excreted body fluids.

"With every step I took, every hour I stayed there, every order I obeyed, the will to live seemed to slip further away, and despair eased its way in and usurped hope's place. I prayed we would be evacuated.

"And then Sister Miriam fell ill. She keeled over while tending a patient, and within hours was delirious, with an incredibly high fever and recurrent vomiting. She was semi-conscious and couldn't recognize anyone, but kept calling for water, over and over again. The doctors shook their heads helplessly and said that there was little we could do except wait.

"I had seldom prayed before, but I prayed then—and swore, too, ordering God not to let anything happen to my friend. The next day I came down with the same fever. I collapsed, just as Sister Miriam had, and it was two days before I woke up again, not understanding what had happened. I heard voices, sounding very hesitant and afraid. I opened my eyes, and saw Helen and Magda standing by my bed. They were my co-workers, had attended the same college and arrived in Africa on the same flight I did. I had thought they were my friends. But now I saw, by the look on their faces, that they were afraid of me. And I didn't know why.

"'Tell me what's happened.' I tried to talk through lips so dry they felt burned. But Magda and Helen didn't answer. I struggled to sit up, and realized that I must have vomited all over the ragged hospital gown I was dressed in instead of my uniform, and all over my bed.

"I remembered, then. 'How's Sister Miriam?' They looked away, and I realized without needing to be told, that my friend was dead. A cold and furious anger welled up within me.

How could she be dead? I had treated so many sick and dying people, but I was only twenty-four. I had never lost a friend. Not someone close to me, someone I thought of as family in addition to friend.

"I pulled myself up off the bed, and shakily stood up. I wanted to cry or to scream, to lash out at Magda and Helen, who were still standing there, or God or anyone, in retaliation for losing my friend. I focused my anger instead on my soiled nightgown. 'Magda. I don't know how long I've been sick, but I need some clean clothes. Can you bring them to me? I don't know if I can make it down the hall by myself.'

"Both nurses had turned their backs and were walking away. 'What's the matter with you? I'm telling you I need a change of clothes.' Helen looked over her shoulder. Her face was a study in fear and futility. 'There aren't any more clean gowns,' she stuttered. 'There isn't any more of anything. The hospital has run out of supplies. We're going to be evacuated tomorrow.' 'There are troops on the way,' Magda added. "To suppress the fighting, and take us out of here.'

"'Then let me have my uniform back,' I demanded, exasperated by their unwillingness to help. 'Bring me my uniform, or tell me where it is and I'll get it myself!'

"At that moment, Ursula walked into the room, and the two nurses fled out the door. The head nurse looked as angry as I felt. 'Lie down, and stop shouting!' she ordered. 'I can hear you all over the hospital. Do you know that you've been clawing and screaming at anyone who tried to touch you, for the past two days?' 'I want clean clothes,' I repeated stubbornly.

"'We couldn't change you, because you fought so hard. And there hasn't been time. I don't know where your uniform is; you were sick and it was taken away the morning we put you to bed. If you want another uniform, you'll have to find it yourself—I just don't have the time to hunt for supplies, when there's so much else to do, getting ready to leave here. All these patients have to be mobilized.'

She frowned.

"'The doctors say you passed the crisis last night, and you're going to recover. I'm sorry about Sister Miriam.'

She shook her head. 'You've guessed, haven't you?' I nodded, numbly.

"'Look around, and try to see other people the way that she did. And then decide if she would want you to go on feeling sorry for yourself when so many people in this hospital need your help.' And she turned around abruptly and stalked out.

"I don't know what I had expected her to say, but her last words hurt immeasurably. Though they didn't make me change my attitude. I decided that, even if no one had time to help me, I was going to find something to wear—a clean uniform; a gown, street clothes, anything. I was not going to dwell on my shortcomings;

the gospel according to Ursula.

"I leaned against the wall of the corridor, then began to stagger down the hall. I was still feverish, and it seemed to me as I stumbled over and around human bodies lining the corridor that I was walking through some incarnation of Dante's inferno. Everywhere I went people held out their hands, or cried incoherently, or stared apathetically at the floor. The smell was nauseating, and the sights and sounds I encountered were beyond belief.

"I turned a corner, went down another hallway toward the primitive little operating room with its smell of old, dried blood and disinfectant. I stood in the middle of the floor and added my voice to the general babble, to the voices of all the sick and dying human beings jammed together into too confined a space.

"I started swearing, and I didn't care who heard me or what I said. 'All I want is my clothes! Please somebody, just give me the damn clothes!' No face met mine. Eyes turned inwards, their owners' thoughts distracted by despair. I opened my mouth to scream, and a groan came out. I swore again.

"Then I saw her. She was leaning against the far wall, wedged into a corner and surrounded by other people on all sides. She was a tiny, dark skinned woman, so small that at first, in the dim light of the hallway I mistook her for a child. But when I drew closer I could see that she was probably in her thirties, though her wrinkled forehead and fingers gave her the ancient, knowing appearance of someone much older. She was wearing a dirty, terribly ragged but gaudily bright orange bathrobe.

A child's robe, which still seemed too large for her short, slender frame. She said something, in a language I didn't understand, and I realized she was beckoning to me. She wanted my attention. I stepped closer to her.

"You must realize that I was starved for color in a world which had robbed my senses of it for so long. And the orange of her robe drew me forward in fascination. It took a moment to realize she was holding something out, with the hand that beckoned. A brown paper bag, with clothing inside it. I saw the contents, poking through the open top. A dress, underwear, stockings. And an old, but serviceable looking pair of brown shoes.

"I stared at her wonderingly, as she smiled, and continued holding out the bag of clothes. Obviously, she wanted me to take them. But where had she found them? Supplies were exhausted, and she wouldn't have had access to the hospital's supply closets, in any case.

"I had been wandering through the hospital, cursing the lack of any clean clothing to wear. But this woman wore nothing except the orange bathrobe and a thin slip underneath. I could see its pale sheen wherever buttons on the robe were missing. She was barefoot; the shoes in the bag were probably the only footwear she owned. I would have sold my soul at that point for clean clothing. Ursula was right; I had been thinking, self-centeredly, of my own needs.

"But clothing, the clothing which was in that brown bag, represented a treasure to the woman in the orange bathrobe. Even if the clothes were too large for her, they supplied a dignity which could make her plight as a refugee more bearable. She owned nothing more personal or more valuable in this world, and yet she was holding the brown bag out to me.

"How much English did she speak? How much of my yelling and cursing had she understood? I was ashamed. But covetous, too. I touched the brown bag, tentatively. The woman in orange moved away from the wall, and turned toward me. I gasped. The clothes fell out of the bag and I caught them in my hands. With both my hands. The woman in orange could not catch them, for her left arm ended in an empty sleeve. Her right hand, arm, and eye were intact and normal. But the stump of her left arm ended at the shoulder, and what should have been her left eye was a closed, unseeing lump within the deeply gouged scar tissue of her face.

"She smiled at me, with the right side of her face, which was kind and caring. There were no wounds. Her deformity was not caused by the ongoing war, but by birth defect or an accident, long ago.

"I stood there numbly, holding onto what was now a jumbled heap of clothes, and the woman reached out and handed me the brown paper bag, with her right hand. I think something broke inside me then. I lost confidence in my own infallibility, if nothing else. I'd grown up in Harlem, and I thought I'd learned to fight back against injustice, poverty and prejudice. But when I looked at this woman, I realized that I understood so little. I didn't know, up until that moment, what it means to be broken. To be broken to bear. But the woman in orange knew. And was still so ready and willing to offer a gift.

"I mumbled something. 'Thank you,' I suppose, and I stuffed the clothing back into the brown paper bag. And then I ran away. I'm not proud of that, but I couldn't face her, regarding me so calmly and with such sadness in her one good eye. I found another corner, in a different hallway, where there were fewer people. And there, not caring if anyone saw me, I changed into my new, clean clothes."

Sister Monica wipes the sweat off her forehead, and sighs.

"I never saw that woman in orange again. The hospital was evacuated and I was transferred to another hospital in a different part of Africa. Later I came back to the United States and worked as a nurse in western New York state. Then—and it took me a while to get up the courage to do this—I wrote to Sister Miriam's order, which had a convent near where I was living. It took even longer to realize I had a vocation, but whenever I doubted myself, or distrusted God, I would close my eyes and remember her again, the woman in orange."

She shuts her eyes, as if to call the image back once again.

"Perhaps she stole the clothes. Perhaps someone gave them to her, or she found them. I don't know. They were just old clothes."

She opens her eyes.

"I'm only joking when I talk about being 'God's thief,' you know. It isn't possible to 'steal' God's love. Not when God has given it to you. Though of course there are people who will try to take it away, or tell you that you don't deserve to be loved."

She pauses, and then continues,

"But when I meet people who think they aren't, and

never have been loved, I do my best to find something for them. Even if it's only an alarm clock or a pile of old clothes."

We leave the storeroom and the basement of the church, step outside and see the clouds above the steeple breaking apart, like a pair of outstretched hands, making way for the fast-spreading orange of the noonday sun.

Gift

There's a woman in the park
stealing food from a garbage can—
She's sifting through the contents
to live as best she can—
And I don't know why she has to live
that way;
But just like her I've been a thief—
Not of money, but of grief,
For love turns into despair
when it's snatched away.

So I'm stealing love,
bits and pieces of love—
To give away for nothing if I can—
Though all my life I've been a thief—
Not of money, but of grief,
Love heals people when people
give it away.

Eucharist

Sunbeams
chasing shoes down a hard wooden floor . . .
Dust-motes quivering against revolving ankles
Shuffling prayer-pages rustle an old-fashioned grace.
Holy, Holy, Holy . . .

And as worshipers murmur of sin and forgiveness strange ghosts
enter church doors unbidden and mingle the silence of their wounds
with words spilling forth from the comfortable middle-class pews—
frail shopping-bag ladies with disheveled hair, torn dresses
bloat-bellied children whose thin-eaten smiles pucker hollow
making sadness a cry.

Old men with dull eyes, stale whiskers and alcohol breath
turn Quiet to mockery—
What are they doing in God's house?
Who gave them permission to enter?
Even their ghosts should not enter, say a few—
But Quiet accepts outcasts too.
Father, Son, and Holy Spirit . . .
the Bread and Wine feeding their hunger.

And wind-currents shudder the candles while all eyes are lifted
Hymn notes tremble high on a cross, up a carpeted aisle
But memories of pain, old pain, (Christ's death?)
go on bleeding, reopening
Healing and hurting and healing and hurting again.
"Peace which the world cannot give . . ."
Till doors are thrown open—
"I give to you."
Peace, Peace, Peace . . .
"I leave with you."

A Rainy Day

"I'm glad, really glad, you're writing again," Father Joseph says.

He hands back the poem I've shown him. "A Poem Called 'Lost.'"

"I'm trying. The words get stuck, like a jar lid when it's been screwed on too tight."

"Keep trying. The words aren't at fault; it's the feelings they're letting loose which seem so scary."

"And the memories."

I've been part of St. Jude's congregation for more than a year. It's June, and as I look out the window of Father Joseph's office, a light, unhurried summer rain is falling. Drops leave tracks in the dust on the outside pane, as puddles lengthen and drip off the windowsill.

A woman across the street makes uncertain progress, juggling two bags of groceries, her purse and an umbrella. She heaves her way up the steps of an apartment building, where a door opens only after she has pushed the outside buzzer a dozen times. Either she lives there, but doesn't want to fumble for her key, or she is a Good Samaritan carrying groceries to somebody else, this rainy day.

"Why don't you write about the rain?" Father Joseph suggests.

"About the groceries. Maybe . . ." I hesitate, remembering other groceries, irremovably become part of a station wagon's rear-seat upholstery.

We listen to the peals and squeals of automobile and truck tires on wet pavement, and the bellow of each passing semi's brakes, as drivers pause for a red light or oncoming traffic. I say that the brakes sound like humpback whales greeting each other in a heavy sea.

"Write about the rain, the groceries, the lady, and the whales," Father Joseph says.

Whales

Why won't it stop raining?

On this day when I'm carrying home
bacon and cat food and eggs.
God doesn't seem very interested
in ordering it to stop, or even
in sending a friend down the street
to share an umbrella.
My shoes make burping noises. And now the raindrops
are running in swift little rivers off the end of my nose.
I swipe at my face as the mailman
brakes his van to a halt in front of my box.
"Weather for ducks," he says. And
thrusts a damp arm out, inserts a letter. Sleeve damper now . . .
He slams the mailbox shut, puts the flag up, waves, grins.
I grin back. Wave back. Shielding my groceries from the rain
with a wet puckered hand.
"For deep sea creatures."

And I hear it, then.
Way off in the distance, on rain-slick pavement—
a semi's brakes, bellowing.
Echoing—
like the lonely, lost
lovesick and doleful calls
of humpback whales.

Trash Day

"I'm glad you're writing again," Sister Monica says.

"I'm trying," I tell her. "I'm wondering what I should say about Hawley."

She thinks for a moment.

"A poem called lost," she says softly.

I know that she means Hawley, not the manuscript I've shown her.

"I don't think anyone else would use that analogy. Seeing Hawley's life as a 'poem.' I understand, though."

We are standing on the front steps of the church, and enjoying the bright June morning which is a follow-up to two full days of rain. We are waiting for Hawley to finish playing his harmonica. To leave his basement room, lock the door, and come and join us on our morning walk.

Hawley's room is the only one in the church which is ever locked. Not because he owns anything an intruder would consider valuable, but because, as Tall Monica says, "he needs the right to say 'yes and no' to people and to keep himself to himself, just as you and I do."

"He heard me call," she says. "He'll be ready in a minute. He loves trash day."

This is the day of the week when people set their garbage cans by the curb, to be emptied the next afternoon. Sister Monica and Hawley never miss this chance to walk and survey, to see if anything is being thrown out which she can repair, convert, recycle or find a new home for.

Her rules about "collection" are strict—we will wear gloves and touch no items except those piled outside or on top of the trash. Hawley is allowed to retrieve soft drink cans and turn them in for their refundable deposit. The garbage cans and tied bags of trash we leave alone.

Hawley himself was a throwaway before Sister Monica heard his harmonica echoing eerily out of the ground, and coaxed him into exchanging his dark sub-basement below an abandoned dry cleaning store for the old recreation room next to her storage room in the basement of St. Jude's.

"Even Father Joseph wasn't sure it was a good idea," she says. "But I couldn't leave Hawley by himself, now could I? Living in a hole, wandering around at night, stealing food from dumpsters; his next home might have been jail, or a psychiatric hospital, if he'd gone on living out on the street."

She does not know who Hawley really is. No one does. Not Social Services or the police or any of the street people who have their own ways of finding out information.

One day Hawley wasn't living in this neighborhood, and the next he was. Sister Monica doesn't know if "Hawley," which is all he's ever called himself, is a first name, last name, or (with Hawley's garbled speech) a mispronunciation of another name.

"It might be 'Harley,'" Sister Monica says. "But I thought it was easier to pronounce his name the way he says it himself."

Hawley had an existence somewhere, before St. Jude's

or Sister Monica or even the dry cleaning store. But if he remembers a previous identity he can't, or won't, talk about it.

There are scars on his back and shoulders, some recent, some which appear to have been there since early childhood. The person or persons who abandoned him on Keeler Street may or may not be the same who inflicted the ugly, crisscrossed red scars.

Perhaps, as Father Joseph believes, Hawley is satisfied being who he is now and doesn't want to remember who he once was. Darkness, to him, being equated far more with other human beings than a hole in the ground.

We hear thuds leading up from the basement to the vestibule, and know that Hawley is coming up the stairs.

In the Dark

No safety for me
in lighted room—
Where people mingle
and gossip wounds—
No solace for me
in sunlit rooms.

My hiding place
is a sealed off room—
Where no threat enters
no punishment looms—
I find my safety
in darkened rooms.

Hawley

Hawley bounds up the stairs, like some strangely antithetical image of Quasimodo. His bald head bobs up first, then the rest of him, grinning face and enormous body dressed in wrinkled brown slacks and a long sleeved purple tee shirt. He insists on wearing long sleeves, except in the hottest weather. To hide the scars, Sister Monica believes.

He has in the past tried to hide himself, and this is hugely difficult for a man as enormous as Hawley. He is six feet, eight inches tall and weighs more than three hundred pounds. He is in his late teens or early twenties, and has a peaceful and benevolent disposition unless his rules are broken. He has only two rules: no one does harm to the church or to Sister Monica.

When she convinced Father Joseph to let Hawley come and live in the basement of St. Jude's, he agreed at least in part because she thought it would stop any ongoing vandalism, and this has proved to be the case. Hawley is now the sexton, custodian, and night watchman of St. Jude's, and would-be intruders have learned to stay away. As Kenneth, a young street hustler who is an occasional visitor to the youth group, says, "He's one big dude." Kenneth has a friend who made the mistake, late one ill-fated night, of trying to scrawl graffiti on a wall in the sanctuary. Hawley materialized behind him in the darkness, and as Kenneth explained later, "The Big Man didn't throw Shotgun out. Shotgun let himself out, ninety miles an hour. He ran so fast he was three miles away before he ever slowed down. He shook and shook next day, like he'd had a bad trip or seen the devil, and I guess he thought maybe he did."

Hawley, for his part, doesn't seem to mind what people think about him as long as they leave him alone. He gets along politely, if somewhat warily, with the teenagers in the youth group who have long since stopped referring to him behind his back as "Crawley Hawley." The change of attitude came about when Anthea (Mrs. Thea), their advisor, drill sergeant and best friend, began showing them video tapes of "Beauty and the Beast." Not the animated fairy tale, but a 1980s TV series which features a character half lion, half man who lives with other outcasts in a subway.

"For someone so ugly, Hawley's okay," Kenneth's brother Sidney says in a display of open-mindedness.

Sometimes, when the youth group meets at night in the old, sprawling kitchen of St. Jude's, Hawley sits at the edge of the room, as close to the exit as he can get, and listens while Anthea encourages the kids to talk about religion, politics, sports, sex, personal issues—anything which feels important to them. Hawley pays attention, though he doesn't join in.

Then he'll go back to his own room, and play his harmonica, not tunefully, but loudly enough sometimes that the sound drifts up through the heating pipes and is carried all over the church. Occasionally, his playing interrupts Father Joseph's sermon, or accompanies parts of the liturgy on Sunday morning.

Hawley enjoys keeping the church clean and going with Sister Monica on her various expeditions. He is paid for his work, and Sister Monica oversees cooking lessons on the antiquated stove in the kitchen, and is guide and companion on trips to the bank, the grocery store and the laundromat. Father Joseph has had a shower installed in one of the two bathrooms in the basement, and has reserved it for Hawley's use, changing the sign on the other bathroom door to indicate its continued availability to everyone else. With his own bedroom and a bathroom down the hall, Hawley is at peace with all the world.

Still, the only person he'll say more than a few words to at a time is Sister Monica, whom he adores.

"Gram," he calls her. Or, "Monka."

"Does he think I'm his grandmother?" Sister Monica often wonders. "Did he have a grandmother, who was kind to him, even when someone else was abusing him? I don't know why he calls me that, but I'm glad he trusts me."

I do not tell her that deacons, nuns, and grandmothers have some qualities in common which may comfort even someone as lost as Hawley.

"I don't believe he's mentally retarded," she insists. "He picks up on so many things, so quickly. But he's been hurt and abused—maybe he's brain damaged, or perhaps his mind just decided to shut itself down. I hope he'll tell me who he is, someday. He has a chance to live independently if he's taught the right skills."

Hawley spends part of each week at a sheltered

workshop, where he earns additional money, gets therapy, and is learning to be more comfortable dealing with people.

Wednesday, though, is his day to go "collecting" with Sister Monica.

Now, as he joins us on the steps, he hesitates, noticing me, then turns to his friend to ask a question.

"Walk," he demands. "Walk?"

"Yes, Hawley, we are," Sister Monica assures him. She hands him a canvas backpack, and has already given me a similar backpack and a pair of plastic gloves. (There are no gloves big enough to accommodate Hawley's slab-sized fists.)

She dons gloves herself and shoulders her own bag.

"Remember, we don't dig in the trash and we don't touch food," she says, as we set off down Keeler street. "It was hard for me to make Hawley understand, when we first started 'collecting,' that he couldn't eat out of the garbage cans anymore, and that he didn't need to scare off anyone who tried to say hello. He's come a long way in three years."

We walk slowly along Keeler where the sidewalk is buckled and overgrown with grass, and adjoining houses are wood frame, usually single story, and some falling down. This is a neighborhood of elderly, poor and working class people, some of whom own their own homes but are living on fixed incomes and have no money to spend on paint or new siding or repairing leaky plumbing or lost shingles.

New trash has blown on top of old trash already littering front yards; the gaseous-greasy odor of garbage heating in the noonday sun is accompanied by the fierce, on-off buzzing on an ever-circling, ever-landing swarm of kamikaze flies.

We will walk north on Keeler for six blocks, then turn right onto Estes and circle the block, coming back to St. Jude's in an hour with our bags of "treasure."

We scan the piled trash for furniture, books or appliances which look salvageable. Smaller items can be added to our backpacks; the heavier items Sister Monica will return for later on, in her pickup truck, with Hawley and Father Joseph to help out.

"I found a small stove, once," Tall Monica says. "Took it down to the appliance store near where I live, and the manager fixed it as a Christmas gift, no charge. Made a family very happy that Christmas Eve."

We go on walking down the street.

I think what stares we would attract, if there were anyone around to stare, though for the moment Keeler Street seems abandoned. The tiny, elderly, African American nun, the hulking, mentally handicapped young white man, and myself. Scavengers.

Before we reach the second block, Hawley has found a box of blankets which are clean and nearly new, and a bag of hard-cover Reader's Digest condensed books.

"Large print," Sister Monica says. "Perfect for the nursing home."

We divide the blankets and books among our backpacks.

A few minutes later she crows over the discovery of some old glass jelly jars, with lids which aren't yet rusty and can be sterilized and reused.

"You wouldn't believe the things some people throw away," Tall Monica sighs. "Even in a neighborhood like this where people don't have much money. You wouldn't expect to see unopened cans of food in the trash, but look." She points out a paper bag containing untouched cans of fruit cocktail and spaghetti sauce.

"More people go to the soup kitchens and the food banks now, instead of risking food poisoning eating out of the trash. Still, I always hate seeing the waste."

She makes note of a battered old television set with a broken antenna, and a bookcase with two missing shelves.

"I'll come back for those later."

We walk down the street a little farther.

"Hawley used to live in that old building over there," Sister Monica says, pointing out the ruins of a store still marked "Cleaner's" next to an abandoned mini-mall.

"It's hard for me to imagine living underground and being afraid to come out," she says. "But for someone Hawley's size to be forced to make himself disappear—what did that do to his self esteem? He couldn't be invisible, but someone certainly wanted him out of the way."

She stops as we find a few empty video cassette tape plastic cases on the ground, and put them in our backpacks.

"Maybe he got too big for someone to handle, or control any more," I say, thinking out loud. "They were afraid to hit him and didn't want to care for him, so they dropped him off here, in an unknown neighborhood."

She nods.

"It has to be something like that. Or he ran away when the people in charge of his life were just passing through. Have you ever seen the marks on his back?"

I haven't, but remember how she has described the appalling red scars.

"They didn't just beat him, I think." She looks at Hawley unhappily. "He isn't afraid of most things, though he's shy around people and always wants to get back inside a building if it starts to thunder. Otherwise he doesn't mind loud noises. But I found out the hard way; he's scared to death of an iron."

Hawley has been lagging behind us, as he always does when anyone else comes along on his walks with Sister Monica, though she orders and cajoles him to keep pace with her. Sometimes he will, if they are alone, but almost never when they are accompanied. Now she tries again.

"Walk with us, Hawley. Friends walk together. Don't hang back as if you're afraid of people."

This time he surprises us both, and does come up.

"Home?" He points to the dry cleaning building. "Home."

"Not any more, Hawley," Sister Monica says. "Not home. Never again."

But Hawley waves a hand, points at the ground, then shields his eyes against the sun.

Sister Monica understands his gestures better than anyone. She translates for me while focusing her attention upon Hawley.

"Yes, I know. It must have been very dark, no sunlight at all when you lived underground. And I think you were very brave, first to live under the ground, and then to come up again when we asked you to."

"Jahn. Jahn." Hawley is still gesturing with his hands, and trying very hard to explain.

"Jahn."

Sister Monica looks startled and then she beams, a smile spreading broadly across her face.

"Yes, Hawley! Yes, that's very good. You've remembered the Bible study, haven't you? Father Joseph and Mrs. Thea will be proud of you."

"What did he say?" I ask.

"'John.' The Gospel of John.We had a Bible study at the church, yesterday afternoon. Hawley sat on the floor and listened. We were talking about John 1.5."

She pauses, wonderingly.

"Hawley must have remembered that discussion when he saw his old hiding place."

She smiles at Hawley. Tired of waiting for us to stop talking and go back to "collecting," he takes his harmonica out and begins to play. Something much quieter this time, with sweet soft harmony.

"John 1.5?" I ask.

"The light shines in the darkness," Sister Monica says. "And the darkness has not overcome it."

Recycling

The recyclers have arrived to reclaim the trash—
newspapers, egg cartons, milk jugs,
aluminum cans—
There are special bins set by the curb and their contents
earmarked
for descent through the crusher and eventual
resurrection.

The recyclers are hauling away
any items which can be made new,
except of course they will not take away
the people who frequent the trash
and are throwaways, too.

The women and children and men
who depend for their lives on the refuse
in garbage cans—
must wait until strangers who salvage the garbage
depart
to come back to dumpsites where laws have forbidden
their trespass.

They will steal what no one else can use;

They are people who, themselves, have been refused.
Lungs breathing, hearts beating,
somehow they survive another day—
Should they wait to be recycled like cardboard boxes?

Or have their foreheads stamped
"redeemable"
like soda cans.

Fred and Jerry

"I'm worried about Fred and Jerry," Sister Monica says.

Fred and Jerry are the two old men who play checkers on St. Jude's altar in the afternoons.

"Fred needs cataracts removed from both his eyes," Father Joseph explains. "But he's been refusing to schedule the operation. It's outpatient surgery, but he doesn't think he'll be able to put any drops in his eyes, afterwards. Jerry would do it for him, but his memory is terrible. He gets confused. Fred is afraid that if this surgery takes place, he won't be well enough to take care of Jerry, and Jerry won't know how to take care of him."

"Jerry is eighty-seven and Fred is eighty-five," Sister Monica says. "And they're each totally dependent upon the other."

"Aren't there organizations which can help them?" I ask.

"Of course," Sister Monica says. "I've told them that. They also have enough money to hire someone to come in. But they don't want outsiders 'bothering' them. That's how they feel."

"It isn't just the eye surgery," Father Joseph says. "What will happen if Jerry has to go into a nursing home? He loses his temper more often, now. What happens when

Fred can't manage him at home? And if Fred becomes disabled then Jerry can't cope."

"Fred really needs this surgery," Sister Monica says. "Without it he'll lose all his vision. He can only see a little out of the right eye none at all out of the left."

"Talk to him again," Father Joseph says. "I will, too. Maybe he'll change his mind."

"They can't stop getting old, though, can they?" Sister Monica says. "I don't read print so easily myself these day. I think it's as confusing as adolescence, this 'getting older.' Your body doesn't do what it's told, the rules keep changing, and any sense of security goes out the window."

At forty-four, I can't imagine what it is like to be eighty-five. And I wonder if Fred, Sister Monica, Jerry or even Father Joseph can remember what it was like to be sixteen, or forty-three.

I'm Getting Older

I'm older now.
Not old, you understand—
but getting older.
It's been a while
since I could leap the steps
three at a time.
I have to scratch that one small itch
in the center of my back
with a bent coat hanger—

I'm getting older.
The toilet claims
a great deal of my time,
and sometimes I will pretend to be soundly asleep—
to avoid conversation. It isn't my fault—
people say that I
am getting older.

I don't always hear when the telephone's
ringing—
And even the weatherman speaks in a language
I don't understand.
His forecasts are wrong just as often,
but now he uses—
computer generated graphics
to make the clouds dance wildly
in a plastic sky.

And I—I
am getting older.
Relatives think that they know what is best
for me—

They tell me when to eat
and what to wear—
who to ask over for dinner,
and have they been
widowed or divorced and how recently—?
I listen to commercials and wonder if I should
purchase additional life
insurance,
renew subscriptions to all my magazines,
or write out a living will
getting ready for dying.

And yes, it is true
that I am getting older—
These days it takes longer
to leave my chair;
the doctor has told me
I ought to cut back on caffeine.

I'm older, but oh—
how I still love to see the morning sun,
shining through pulled back drapes,
first thing upon rising—
and as I make fresh coffee
in a chipped old pot,
I can hear the birds outside demanding,
'who-are-you? who-are-you?'
in the willow tree beyond
my kitchen window.

And though there is no reprieve, I do not mind
growing older if life will continue so full of surprises—
surprises which have been, and are, the best part of a life
like mine.

Christine

"Get lost. Get lost."

Christine's thin, childish voice is only a whisper, but it echoes in the quietness of the church as the few people still lingering past the conclusion of the Sunday morning service make their way through the front doors and down the steps.

It is a hot, humid, early July morning.

"Going home for Christmas!"

Christine pays no attention to me, standing by her side. She is talking to Jesus in his faded brown robe in the middle of the Good Shepherd window.

"Five, four?" she says. "Five, four. Four, five.

She turns my way, but her eyes do not find mine. Her pale blond hair falls in limp, long strands over her shoulders. She rocks back and forth on her left foot; her right foot is tucked, stork fashion, behind her left knee. She turns to the window again to initiate another conversation with Jesus, and she wiggles her fingers in and out through a shaft of sunlight working its way through a crack in the stained glass border.

"Going home for Christmas."

Christine's mother, who has spent the last five minutes apologizing to Father Joseph for an incident Christine caused at this morning's service, is hurrying our way.

"Christine. Church is over. It's time to go home."

Christine continues whispering to the window.

"Five more minutes, and then we're on our way."

Caroline glances at me, and shrugs. We step back to wait. With Christine, we both know that transitions sometimes take a little time.

"I am so sorry about what happened." Caroline's voice is almost as thin and breathless as Christine's, though in appearance she is the mutt-and-jeff opposite of her daughter; brunette where Christine is blond, short and stocky in contrast to Christine's slimness.

"She doesn't usually misbehave during communion," Caroline says. "I don't know what made her so upset."

Little Monica, the church organist, walks up and joins us. She is a tall, gaunt, grey-haired woman with hair tied back in a bun. She is Christine's godmother. Father Joseph baptized Christine three years ago, and Little Monica, who has known the family for a long time, asked to sponsor her.

Little Monica isn't as severe as she looks, though she has never been afraid to venture an opinion.

But she loves Christine, and is never upset by her behavior.

"It wasn't your fault, Caroline," she says now. "I played a different offertory hymn, not the one she heard the last time she was here. I should have stayed with 'Praise God from Whom All Blessings Flow.' She likes that."

"It's no excuse for throwing her bread down the aisle," Caroline says.

Christine continues to wiggle her fingers up and

down against the window while ignoring us all.

She is Hawley's age, but unlike him, makes no attempt to enter or explore our world. She is content to create and exist in a world of her own.

She has never said her mother's name, or her own. 'Four, five, five, four,' and 'Get lost! Going home for Christmas!' are the only phrases Christine has ever used.

"Like having a parrot in the house," her mother sometimes protests. But Caroline, a single parent who knows how difficult life can be raising her autistic child all alone, has only once tried to institutionalize Christine.

"I put her in a private hospital when she was fifteen. Spent half my ex-husband's income to do it," she explained. "It was supposed to be a decent place. I went to visit a week later and there were bruises on her arms and legs. Like someone had knocked the heck out of her. I made a fuss and they told me that she'd had a couple of falls. Well, I know Christine has problems, but she could probably walk a tightrope if I let her. Balance isn't an area where she's lacking. So I decided that since she's always been fairly well behaved, and doesn't try to hurt herself, the house, or me, there's no good reason not to keep her at home. She's happier than she would be somewhere else, and I'm happy knowing she's safe and not being abused."

Christine's father still sends money for her care, though he hasn't been to see her for several years.

"Not his fault," Caroline says. "He does love her, but he couldn't take the pressure, that 'five, four, five, four,' all the time, and having her look right through him. He's good about helping with bills; otherwise I'd never be able to manage. Not working part time instead of full time when she's at the mental health center."

Christine attends the same sheltered workshop as Hawley, but on different days. She never seems to care where she is or what day it is. The windows at St. Jude's are an entertainment for her, and her mother attends church, at least in part, because it gives them both a break from each other. Christine is usually quiet and well behaved if allowed to drift up and down, touching the stained glass windows.

This morning's contretemps was a rare occurrence.

Christine's mother will let her walk back and forth between the windows, until it is time to receive communion, when she goes and takes her daughter by the hand, and leads her to stand by the altar. Christine never resists, but perhaps this morning, as Little Monica thinks, the offertory hymn really did upset her. She sulked and hung back on the trip up the aisle, causing Caroline to increase the pressure on her hand. When Father Joseph approached with her bit of home-baked bread, instead of accepting it and cramming it eagerly into her mouth as she usually does, Christine flailed away from Caroline's side, seized the bread, and flung it down the aisle.

There was an instantaneous, pained, and barely suppressed gasp from the twenty-plus parishioners standing and kneeling around the altar.

"Get lost!" Christine sang out. "Get lost! Going home for Christmas!"

She turned and ran to the back of the church.

Little Monica, who had just finished receiving her

own communion, hurried back to the organ and began to play "Amazing Grace," which is a hymn Christine loves.

Sister Monica, serving in her capacity as deacon, slipped down and picked up the bread from the edge of the carpet. She followed Father Joseph and continued to administer the chalice, as he went unperturbably on, dispensing the bread.

Caroline walked determinedly back down the aisle, took Christine's hand, and led her once again toward the altar. This time she received without incident, to her mother's relief.

"Just because she usually behaves, doesn't mean she always will," Caroline says now. "It's the times she doesn't behave that put all the grey hairs on my head. Like yesterday afternoon. I'd gone into my room to take a nap, and she was fine, listening to music like she always does, and then she couldn't find something she wanted in the refrigerator and so, of course, decided to throw everything in the fridge out her bedroom window. By the time I woke up, most of our food was on the sidewalk. Luckily, it's a one story house; I managed to save a few things that didn't get broken."

She laughs. "Living with her definitely isn't dull."

She puts a hand on her daughter's elbow.

"Five minutes is up, Christine," she says in a voice not meant to be disobeyed.

Christine recognizes her mother's tone and disengages, obediently, from the window, but not before giving one last farewell pat to Jesus' shoulder.

"Five, four. Four, five. Going home for Christmas!"

"I wish you knew how to say 'goodbye'," Little Monica says, wistfully.

She takes off her old fashioned, non-digital wrist watch, and lets Christine hold its softly ticking presence next to her ear, as we walk through the vestibule together.

"I don't even try to ask 'why', any more," Caroline says, as we move toward the doors.

"They can talk and talk about all the new research being done on autism. That's just fine—I'm glad they're trying so hard to figure it out. I have to take care of Christine, and all I know is that she's never said my name. She's twenty years old and her favorite television program is Sesame Street, and last week she tried to shampoo her hair with a box of saltine crackers. Let the researchers tell me something I don't know about autism, after living with it for twenty years."

Little Monica is humming, for Christine's benefit.

"Amazing grace, how sweet the sound."

"Four, five," Christine says. "Five, four."

"Going home for Christmas!" Caroline and I both exclaim, and then burst out laughing. Little Monica laughs too, and we walk out of the church into the sunshine.

Four, five

Four, five—
stay alive.
Good luck trying
to survive.

Five, four—
no more, no more.
Go inside
and lock the door.

Get lost!
Get lost!
Going home
for Christmas.

They Say

Child with strange eyes—
hopeless, they say
Will you ever return
to our world to play?
You, who snatch sunlight
out of the air
And weave it through ends
of your long, tangled hair—
You, who are beautiful
and far away
Should I believe
you will know me, someday?
Spinning in circles
you rock and you stare
or curl on the floor
next to table and chair—
You scream without warning
and push me away
What help can I give you—
what prayers should I pray?
Child, lost child
though you may not care
how I feel about you—
my love is still there.

Little Monica

Christine bangs loudly on the keys of the organ, before jumping up from the bench and running to her favorite spot by the Good Shepherd window.

Little Monica, sitting on the organ bench herself, watches her go, and sighs.

Keisha, a tall, thin, brown skinned girl who looks much younger than her twelve years, edges nervously forward and waits for an invitation, to help play the organ.

"Five minutes of the Bach, then we improvise," Little Monica tells her. "Come on, honey. You already play this thing better than I do."

Together, the tall, grey-haired church organist and the girl who never smiles practice the prelude for the next week's Sunday service. The notes resound from the hundred-year-old organ, which Little Monica keeps in tune. Everyone else in the church stops what they're doing to listen to the music and enjoy.

The church belongs to the youth group on Monday afternoons; between four and five they play Ping-Pong in the basement or chess upon the altar. Today there are two boys and two girls using the chessboards; another boy is sprawled in the middle of the carpeted aisles between pews; he reads a comic book.

At five o'clock, when Anthea (Mrs. Thea, their drill-sergeant, advocate, and mother-for-all-seasons) joins them, they will reconvene in the kitchen in the basement, which they have chosen as their refuge and redecorated to their own taste.

They will stay there till seven or eight, sleeping, snacking, watching video tapes or playing the hand-held video games they've brought with them, and talking to Thea.

Some of them talk all the time. Keisha is much more quiet; if left to herself she would never go downstairs, but would sit behind the organ for hours and hours practicing fugues.

Little Monica is trying to convince her that music, and the playing of music, can be fun.

Today, at least, it seems to be working.

As if reading each other's thoughts (and in fact, they have been practicing the music for weeks) they move smoothly from the Bach into a swift, free-flowing composition of their own devising.

It isn't jazz and it isn't gospel, but a little bit of both, with snatches of classical music from Bach and Beethoven thrown in. It makes me want to cry and stamp my feet at the same time.

"That was terrific!" Little Monica says, when they finally slow down and bring the music to an end. "You won't forget me when you're playing at Carnegie Hall someday, will you honey?"

Keisha says nothing, but her face is flushed with pride.

She sees Anthea entering the sanctuary and with a tiny movement of her hand, apologizes to the organ and

Little Monica for having to go downstairs.

"It's okay," Little Monica says. "You go on ahead with the others. I'll be here next week and we'll play some more. You'll be ready to play for the Sunday service when I go on vacation next month."

Keisha nods and slides away from the bench, then makes her way slowly to the stairs, always walking very close to the wall.

"Won't she be too nervous to play if you're not here?" I ask.

"She'll be all right. She's been brought up to perform. Been playing before audiences since she was five. It's when she isn't playing, or getting ready to play, that she feels so scared."

Little Monica steps out from behind the organ, and slides the cover shut over the organ keys.

"She's been taking music lessons since she was three years old. Attends a private school—I don't know how her family affords that; they don't have very much money. But she has a real gift. She just doesn't know how to have fun."

Little Monica stretches and yawns.

"I know how she feels because I used to be like that. No good at anything (or so I thought) except music. Only my family didn't encourage it." She thinks for a moment.

"I'm sixty-five. When I was growing up women weren't encouraged to follow music as a career. Either you married and raised a family, or lived with your own family while you looked for a sensible job which would bring in some money. I didn't get much of an education—never even finished high school—because my family always made my decisions for me. And there were plenty of factory jobs and sales jobs in the city where I used to live."

She touches the top of the organ, gently.

"I was born in Alabama, but my family moved north when I was only seventeen. I was supposed to start looking for work right after we moved, but that wasn't easy in a new neighborhood, a new city, without anyone to help me find a job, and without a high school diploma." She laughs.

"I didn't get married, and I did find a job after months of trying, in a department store. But I never liked it."

She sees the question on my face.

"No, the store isn't there anymore, it folded, years ago. Anyway, I wasn't very confident, selling high-heeled shoes and ladies underwear. I made too many mistakes—the manager wasn't happy. Oh, she didn't fire me—she was a kind and patient lady. But after a year or two the strain told on me. I started worrying about things—things that didn't always make much sense—like whether the house would burn to the ground while I was gone, or whether my mother and father would move out and leave me."

She stares at the floor.

"It got worse. I guess now they'd say I was suffering from my first episodes of depression. Back then it was simply too embarrassing to admit anything was wrong. When I couldn't get out of bed in the morning and go to work my parents decided I was 'having a turn.' They tried everything from cheap dime store medicines and the recommendations of quack doctors, to begging and threats to cure my 'malingering.' The only thing they didn't do was call a psychiatrist. That cost too much money, and besides, their only daughter couldn't possibly be 'crazy.' In the end, not knowing what else to do, my mother herself went out and found a job to make up for my lost income, and when both my parents went off to work in the morning, I was all by myself in the house."

For a minute she sounds sad.

"I felt safe in the house—for awhile. But then, I'd start to wonder whether mother and dad would ever come back again. I was almost twenty-one by that time and crying like a two-year-old if my parents came home fifteen minutes late."

"What did you do?" I ask.

She doesn't answer right away, but walks over to the altar.

"I didn't like it much when Father Joseph carved the chessboards here," she says. "I thought, why desecrate a sacred thing? But then I remembered what it was like when the world collapsed 'in' on me, and for years after that I couldn't see colors anymore, only shades of grey."

She struggles to explain.

"I wore grey, I insisted that my bedroom walls and ceiling be painted grey; there wasn't any music in my life; if there'd been a piano around, I'd have played 'grey.' And when my family finally gave in and sent me to a hospital for treatment, everything I saw there was grey."

"You were hospitalized?'

"Oh, yes. Depression of the kind I had—still have—doesn't go away. But I was talking about the altar." She runs her fingers across and into two empty, recessed black and white squares.

"I know that 'thinking in black and white' is a metaphor for rigidity, but a 'grey' world such as I saw isn't any less limited. I've been part of St. Jude's congregation for a long time, but so have Fred and Jerry. I began to realize, when I thought about Fred's blindness, that changing the altar might help him to 'see' again. Lift him out of his 'greyness' in the same way music—the music I rediscovered during my last long stay in the hospital—changed me."

She checks her watch.

"I need to go home and let my dog out. I wonder—would you like to eat supper with me? Nothing fancy, just left over chicken and cole slaw, but we'd be able to go on talking."

I accept immediately, and she adds that she'll drive me home. I still take the bus to St. Jude's on occasion, and have done so today, even though last Christmas, for the first time since Daniel's death, I gave in and acquired a small car.

Twenty minutes later, we are sitting in the small, air-conditioned kitchen of the home she has lived in for so long, the home she inherited after her parents died.

Her long-haired dachshund, Peanut, curls up comfortably at my feet. I slip him a piece of warmed up drumstick when I think she isn't looking, but she catches me at it.

"He'll beg from you forever, if you do that."

She thinks back to what we were talking about before leaving the church.

"I didn't cooperate most of the times I was in the hospital."

She waves a chicken wing toward a kitchen window.

"Once I almost severed two fingers when I put my right fist straight through a plate glass window. On an unsecured ward at the hospital—not here. I never broke anything in this house for some reason. But I didn't like being locked up." She shrugs. "I'd be home for a while, start feeling a little better, then refuse to take any more of my medication, get worse for a few days, and wind up right back in the hospital, out of my mind. I was suicidal; had my stomach pumped three or four times. The grey fog all around me never went away. I remember the lowest point in that whole bad time. I was sitting on my bed—my hospital bed, that is—and I was alone in the room because my roommate had been discharged and left for home that same morning. I felt terrible because she'd been allowed to leave and I had to stay. There wasn't a single decoration in the room—not a picture, not a flower, not a book or a bookcase—we weren't allowed to have items which we might destroy. And the whole room was white—the walls, the floor, the ceiling were all white; the sheets and the blanket on the bed, and the robe and the nightgown I wore. White, but to me they appeared grey. I can't explain what that was like, what I'd been going through all those years. When people describe 'hell' as a fiery red, I think 'no, that isn't right, it must be grey.' And I think of hell as a cold, damp, cotton-wool bundled place."

She pushes aside the remains of her chicken dinner.

"Anyway, I was sitting on my bed, and a nurse

opened the door and came in with a med-cart. She needed to give me a shot for some reason—maybe a tetanus booster; I don't remember. There was a needle on top of an ugly metal tray. And suddenly I felt as if I'd stepped outside myself and was experiencing life truthfully for the first time ever. I was looking at the scene in the room as if I'd just dropped down from heaven, from some other planet. And I saw this little, insignificant frightened person—the person that was me—cowering away from a more powerful person, the nurse, and all the time being swallowed by an encroaching cloud of grey. Grey had taken over that room; it had overwhelmed my life, had fogged out any achievements I'd ever valued; had led to separation from friends and family, and now was threatening the small hope for any future I still had."

She smiles.

"I knew in that moment when I saw and felt the grey closing in, that I wanted to love and laugh and hope and make music again—and have fun. But I didn't know how."

She begins to clear away dishes, piling plates in the sink.

"If the nurse had called me 'crazy' to my face right then, I would have agreed with her. But then a miracle happened. The door to my room was still open and someone at the nurses' station way down the hall turned up the radio. They were playing ragtime music. A tune I'd heard before, I suppose, and hadn't noticed. But this time it electrified me."

She whistles as she begins to wash the plates. I help her dry.

"And then another miracle took place. For a moment, the grey fog all around me 'separated.' I don't know any other word to use except that. The fog broke in pieces around me, and I could see color for the first time to years, and the world suddenly changed. There was color in the room I had thought completely grey. A little sunlight filtered past the windowsill. A blue clothing tag was sewed onto the hem of my nightgown. The nurse had a trace of red lipstick, and she was smiling because she liked the music too. I understood, even as she approached with the horrible needle, that she was trying to help, not oppress me. And when she thrust the needle in my arm I didn't fight. I could see a purple napkin on a food tray on a cart out in the hall. I remembered—I could imagine again—what color felt like, even as I experienced the jab of the needle. I remembered a sunset, a sunrise, blue skies, green trees, my mother's old scuffed, orange slippers."

She thrusts a fistful of silverware, dripping, at me.

"Oh, the change didn't last long. Not that time, anyway. The grey came back again off and on for almost two years. But the music had changed something in me that day. I knew that I was going to get well. The greyness had lifted once, and if it could lift that one time it could happen again. I began to go into the dayroom where a shabby old piano occupied one corner, and I sat down at the piano on these daily visits and began to play it. I played and played it every time I had the chance. The other patients liked it, and the nurses didn't mind because I'd started being nicer to them, too. I stopped trying to break windows and hurt myself and agreed to take my medication. Eventually I was diagnosed well enough to go home, and this time I stayed there."

"Didn't you miss the piano?" I ask, as I dry the last dishes.

"I missed it dreadfully, but I played the radio in my bedroom night and day. Later on, after my parents died, I bought myself a piano with some of the money they left me." She points to the Steinway in the hall.

"When the grey went away for good I decided it was time to go out and hunt for a job again, and it wasn't long till I read in the paper that they needed an organist at St. Jude's. I hadn't had training for the organ, though I'd played the piano in the hospital and at school when I was a kid. But I knew I could learn to play their church organ if they gave me the chance. I'm pretty good at teaching myself to play different musical instruments, with just a little bit of instruction. I play the flute and the guitar and can pick out tunes on a lyre, but piano and organ are the instruments I know best."

She helps me find the right cupboards for the rest of the dishes.

"St. Jude's had a fair sized congregation twenty-five years ago. They couldn't find an organist who was willing to work for as little as I would, and I got the job. I didn't care that the pay was low and there weren't any benefits; they were offering me work! Me, a former mental patient! They didn't mind about my illness, as long as I kept taking my medication, and my doctor agreed to give me the go-ahead. I was so proud, after all those years, to have a job!"

We finish the dishes, and proceed to get ready to leave.

"When the congregation drifted away and the church

was sitting empty for a while, of course I couldn't work anymore. But I used to sneak in, even after the church was locked up all the time, because I still had a key to the back door. And I'd go in sometimes and play the organ. I learned how to keep it tuned. Well, almost correctly tuned. It's never been what I consider right—not even when I played it every Sunday. But I didn't want to lose it. Not the organ, or the church, or the music."

She turns to me as we walk towards her car.

"How would Fred and Jerry have felt if I'd complained about the changes to the altar, and then they'd had to give up their checker games? I asked myself that, when I was angry about Father Joseph 'carving up' the altar. I didn't know, of course, that the children would start coming in to play chess—from curiosity, I suppose, but also because playing chess on an altar must seem like a really strange thing for adults to permit them to do! And then I met Keisha."

She shakes her head.

"Like finding myself as a child. But I have to teach her that ragtime isn't a crime."

We climb into her old Volvo. As she starts the engine she adds, "The music was inside me, all those years that I thought I was alone. And music drew me back into the world."

She turns the car radio on, full volume, and plays with the various channels till she finds a jazz station.

"Ragtime," she says emphatically, and long before landing me back at my own front door has convinced me to join her in whistling a Scott Joplin tune.

Songbird (I)

There was once a songbird, caught in the coils of a giant snake, and the snake looked at its victim and said compassionately,

"Don't be afraid—it is only your time, the time which must come to all of us." And the songbird answered,

"I know that, and I am not afraid. But swallow my heart first, because that is where all my music lives, and where all the pain is. Everything else is just silence . . ."

But the snake knew that music is alive in the silence as well, and that the songbird underestimated itself. And the snake swallowed the songbird whole, all at once, and the pain and the music were one meal . . . along with the silence.

A Garden of Extras

"Hi, Meg!" Anthea says, as I join the noisy crowd inside the kitchen. "Grab a chair, sit down over here by me. This is *not* the Garden of Eden, although that's what we're talking about this evening. These kids are telling me what they think went wrong."

She hands me a Pepsi and a bowl of popcorn, and I settle into a tacky, orange and brown recliner with threadbare arms and a footrest arrested half-way to mid-air.

"Donations in the cup on the counter for junk food," Anthea says.

All seven members of the youth group, and a few extras, are here in the kitchen tonight. Hawley sits on the floor in the corridor, his large size forcing him to lean over if he wants to remain outside the room, but still hear what the group is discussing. Christine is here tonight, too, because her mother wanted to go shopping and needed a sitter. Christine drifts in and out of the kitchen, being careful to avoid Hawley. She blows on her fingers or plays with the rainbow-colored Noah's ark magnets which affix a picture of NBA superstar Michael Jordan to the refrigerator door.

The others are used to Christine and pay no attention to her wandering.

Anthea, a fiftyish, African-American woman who is the den-mother to this group, sits in the armchair next to mine. On her left side, lying at the feet of his owner, is an eighth and honorary member of the youth group, a large, black Labrador retriever named "Charlie."

Charlie belongs to Leo, who sits next to Tyrone and Sidney. And on Sidney's left lounges Kenneth, his street-wise and surly older brother, who props his feet up on another chair, and stays as close as he can to the micro-wave oven, open packages of popcorn, and a bag of Snickers bars.

The girls, Keisha, Denise, and Astilbe, have arranged themselves in a shifting and giggling group on the sofa on Anthea's and my right side.

The youth group has long since claimed the entire kitchen as its domain. The walls are hung with posters of rock stars and heroes currently popular within the sports world. The boys rescued the armchairs and the ancient, sagging sofa on which the girls are now sitting, from the alley and brought them inside to create a rec-room. Anthea supplied a few raveling out, braided throw rugs to warm up the scarred, red and white linoleum floor. Between the stove and the refrigerator, both relics of the 1940s, is a modern television and a VCR.

"The Garden of Eden?" I ask.

"We were talking about Adam and Eve," Anthea as-sents, "till I stopped to tell Kenneth I'd throw him out if he keeps stuffing his pockets with the candy bars all of us paid for."

Kenneth, a heavily muscled, white sixteen-year-old who sports a shaved head, multiple earrings and tattoos and a ring in his nose, only leans back in his chair, shrugs, and smirks.

He knows better than to challenge Anthea, who has confronted him on several occasions in the past and won every time.

"He comes to the youth group meetings to compete with Sidney," she explained before I came here tonight. "They may be brothers, but they don't like each other very much, and each one hates it when the other one gets more attention. I'm working on 'em, though. Must be something worth saving about those boys, besides the earrings."

Anthea herself is a large woman, nearly two hundred pounds, with a scarred face, orange tinted hair, and an incredible ability to inspire confidence in others and get things done. She has kicked alcohol and cocaine dependencies, been married and divorced three times, and now lives happily and in perfect cooperation with Ernesto, a quiet and gentle man half her size and ten years younger than she is.

She is ferocious in her defense of St. Jude's youth group.

"They *are* the Bible," she tells me. "Jesus wanted us to stand up for the children."

But the rules she imposes on the youth group are simple and strict.

"They come in drunk or stoned, or try to get high in the church, I throw them out. They fight or start using bad language, I throw them out. They don't backtalk me or run down each other in meetings, and I don't let the noisier ones hog the whole conversation. Other than that, they can say what they please, and they got a safe place here in the meetings to speak their piece. I let them talk out things they're afraid to say even to each other, and then they begin to realize what 'safe' means."

Within the boundaries she lays down, the kids can argue as vociferously as they please.

She has, over the past few months, been encouraging them to put readings from the Bible, which they hear in church, into their own words. Opinions, doubts, independent conclusions follow. And now Tyrone is complaining about Adam and Eve, who in his mind, "messed up."

He is ten years old, African-American and Hispanic, with a divorced father he seldom sees, and a mother who is schizophrenic and spends as much time in mental hospitals as she does at home.

He is plaintively blaming the exile from the garden on Eve.

"Why'd she have to go fooling with that old tree?" he asks. "If she wanted an apple, why didn't she offer to pay God for it? Not grab it when she thinks God ain't looking. I think Eve was just as bad as my mama, when she saw a blouse she wanted at the K-Mart and she stuffed it in her purse, left the store, and got caught shoplifting. Then I'm out of the garden all right, just like Adam. I'm back living with my grandma while Ma's in jail."

One of the three girls sitting on the sofa erupts in protest.

"It wasn't Eve's fault that they got kicked out," Denise says. "She wanted to have a good time, not be so bored, and Adam didn't care how she felt about living in a really boring place—to her, I mean—without any people around, and nothing to do."

Denise is fifteen, white, with dyed blond hair, an excessive amount of make-up and a tendency to flirt. She has run away from home several times, the last time agreeing to go back after receiving counseling at a shelter for teens. Last April, while still only fourteen, she miscarried the child of Dewaller Higgins, a nineteen-year-old high school dropout with a record for stealing cars.

Dewaller, well aware of the fact that Denise's pregnancy could send him to prison, fled the neighborhood despite Denise's avowed plans to marry him and keep the baby.

Now, in July, the miscarriage four months earlier seems forgotten, on her part.

"If Adam treated Eve a little better, she wouldn't have started talking to that dumb snake, " Denise says. "Like my stepmother and my Dad. They fight all the time, but afterwards they go make it up in bed."

She smiles flirtatiously at Leo, a thin, pale, acned adolescent of fifteen, who suffers from shyness and a seemingly permanent drip on the end of his nose. Leo catches her gaze and looks away, embarrassed.

He rests his hand on Charlie's head.

Charlie is Leo's hearing-ear dog. Leo is diagnosed as learning disabled and mildly hearing impaired. He has trouble processing sounds and cannot, for example, discern from the angle a car is approaching, which way he should move to get out of the way, or react to a ringing telephone fast enough to answer it before the ringing stops.

Charlie helps him solve these problems. The dog is also a last-ditch, desperate attempt by Leo's current set of foster parents to keep him from running away. For Leo has run from six other foster homes.

He blows the moisture off his nose into an already sodden Kleenex.

"Maybe God felt about Adam and Eve," Leo says hesitantly, "like Charlie feels about me. Every time I get into trouble Charlie's right there to help me. He does his best to keep me out of trouble, but when I won't listen it's my own fault if I get hurt."

"God isn't a *dog*," Denise says scornfully.

"How do you know?" Tyrone asks.

"She's right about one thing." This is Sidney's contribution. "Adam and Eve could have helped each other more."

"I'd have whipped Eve's ass," Kenneth puts in, glancing Anthea's way to see whether she'll be angry at his comment. Her frown warns him, and he sinks back into his chair.

His father is in jail once again for spousal abuse.

"If Adam had beaten up Eve, God would have thrown both of them out a whole lot sooner," Sidney says. "Remember the landlord where we lived when I was five and you were six, Ken? The guy who broke in and tossed Dad down two flights of stairs for fighting with Ma? Then she called the cops on the landlord."

He shakes his head. He is fifteen, smaller and more peacefully inclined than his brother, though just as opinionated. His hair is combed into matted, pink and blue spikes, and he boasts more earrings than Kenneth, though fewer tattoos.

"I think that if God put 'em into the garden, he

should've taught them how to support themselves. If they were bored, he could have showed them how to make some money. Maybe growing a crop, corn or tobacco, like the pilgrims did, or even a little pot. No police to worry about back then. And God could have showed them a way to sell their stash to all the people who believed in a different religion."

"God isn't a drug dealer!" Denise cries.

"We don't know what was growing in the garden," Sidney says.

I begin to understand that to Kenneth the key to a successful life is intimidation, but to Sidney it is commerce.

"No piano to play in the garden," Keisha says. This is all she says, all evening, and I'm not sure whether she regrets this lack of music in paradise, or is relieved.

"It must have been a very pretty place. Lots of flowers and streams and green trees." Astilbe is eight, too young, really, to be in this group, but she is Tyrone's half-sister and goes everywhere he does. She is intelligent and alert, with a warm, outgoing personality that sheds worry like the sunlight pushing back rain. She brightens a room with her presence, like the small red flowering plant for which she is named.

Her mother, Tyrone's father's second, and also 'ex' wife, is a pretty and frivolous woman with a long succession of boyfriends since the divorce. Astilbe has learned to hide under her bed or in the closet when any of the boyfriends drink too much or become unruly.

"I feel sorry for Adam and Eve," she says. "maybe they didn't understand they were doing something wrong. God was angry because he thought they knew better than to touch things he told them not to, but they really didn't. Like when I went into Mama's bedroom and tried on her make-up. She yelled a lot and made me feel real bad, but she didn't throw me out of the house. God should have yelled at Adam and Eve a lot, too, but not kicked 'em out of the Garden with no place to go."

"Your Mom couldn't throw you out or she'd go to jail," Denise says.

"Nobody's gonna put God in jail," Kenneth points out.

"They put Jesus in jail though, didn't they?" Sidney says. "The Jews or the Romans or somebody put him in jail, and then he got murdered, but he's God so he got to come back again."

"What do you think, Leo?" Anthea asks. "Was God being too tough on Adam and Eve? Did they get what they deserved or should they have been given a second chance?"

Leo shifts in his chair. He looks at Charlie, who stretches, thumps his tail, and yawns.

"I think God must be like Charlie, trying to watch out for me," Leo says. "And maybe like my social worker when she says I'd better listen and listen good."

He sighs.

"She comes to visit and she says, 'Leo, I've found you a real nice placement; parents who really like you and a nice foster home. Now don't run away 'cause if you blow it then you'll wind up in detention, and I just did my best to get you out of there.'" He scratches Charlie's ears, and the dog puts his head on Leo's knee.

"But I don't listen. I get mad or scared or upset about something and I take off down the road, and then the cops pick me up and I'm back in detention. And my social worker says, 'See, Leo, all I wanted was to help you out, and you spoiled it all. You're your own worst enemy.'"

He falls silent, seemingly surprised that he's said so much.

"So Adam and Eve were their own worst enemy?" Anthea asks.

Leo nods.

The others indicate they agree with him.

"What happened, after they got kicked out of the Garden?" Astilbe asks.

"Adam and Eve had to work," Denise says. "They had to pay money for things, after God kicked them out. The kids, the rent, the groceries."

"But they found out that God still loved them," Anthea says. "Even if they were 'their own worst enemy.' God kept coming around, like Leo's social worker, to forgive them and do what he could to make things better."

She looks at her watch.

"We've talked a lot tonight, and it's getting late. We need to clean up; there's popcorn on the floor, and Tyrone, I know you spilled your Pepsi. Putting your comic book over the mess won't hide it from me. You get a paper towel and wipe the floor."

The group addresses itself to sweeping up popcorn and washing and putting away empty popcorn bowls. Anthea gives the rinsed-out Pepsi cans to Hawley so that he can return them for the deposit. He carries the cans to his room, locks himself in, and soon we hear him playing his harmonica.

Christine's mother arrives to take her home. The youth group and Charlie stampede up the basement steps.

Anthea and I exit after them, more slowly.

It is still light outside as I walk to my car, and I see Kenneth and Sidney engaged in a deep conversation with an older man. Astilbe and Tyrone chase each other across the street; they live in different apartments in the same building. Keisha's father is waiting at the curb to drive her home. And to my surprise I see Leo and Denise, escorted by Charlie, heading down the sidewalk together.

"There goes trouble, I'm afraid," Anthea says, coming up behind me, and nodding in the direction of these two teens. "I never imagined that Leo and Denise would get together. I don't want to discourage them if friendship is all Denise is after, but Leo is so gullible he could get into trouble."

She sighs.

"And Kenneth and Sidney are out here, talking to a dealer, only half a block away from the church."

I glance that way but the boys and the older man have disappeared.

"They've gone off somewhere to take care of business," Anthea says. "And there ain't a damn thing I can do about it. I can't get either of those boys to stop using drugs no matter how hard I try."

She looks down the street.

"They're both into pot and amphetamines, and Kenneth has a conviction for selling cocaine."

She rubs the rough, ridged scar below her right cheekbone.

"I don't ever stop worrying about these kids. Maybe because I never had any of my own."

"It sounds as if substance abuse is the serpent in Eden for Kenneth and Sidney."

"You got that right," she says. "It was my devil, too."

She touches the scar again, and I remember her telling me that it was inflicted by her second husband, with the edge of a broken bottle, one night when he was high on crack cocaine.

Free Child

The free child wants
to learn the insides of things—
something about everything
everything about something—
and dreams about being the hero
of unwritten volumes.
But the School says:
"Color between the lines."

The free child wants
to walk by a river at sunrise
play hide and seek with the wind—
learn what songs whales are singing and why
best friends sometimes seem so sad.
But the Church says:
"Save yourself from your sins."

The free child wants
to tower as tall as the stars, or
to tuck up as tiny as individual atoms in
an unexplored galaxy, and then—
to thin, to grow
to flow to some unique, irreplaceable shape . . .
But the World says:
"Learn to fit in."

So who will save the child?
Who will help him grow?
Who will praise the child?
And who will tell her, "No."

And the wise child asks with a shrug
Wary, eyes downcast
"Is anyone out there listening?
Does anyone know who I am?
Is anyone out there watching?
Or just those who don't understand."

Tyrone

Tyrone sits, hunched over, on the front steps of St. Jude's. His hands are fists, and he hides his face between both skinny knees. He sits in the shadows, at the edge of the steps, and Anthea rests beside him in the sun.

He is hiding something, some object which is a problem for Anthea.

I have come upon this scene by accident, and am unsure what is happening between them. I hover nearby, a little embarrassed to be eavesdropping. But they are concentrating so intently on each other that they pay no attention to me.

Anthea wears a voluminous pair of blue sweats, even though it is July and ninety degrees. But she seems cool, unflustered by the heat. Tyrone, on the other hand, is shivering; he wears only his usual thin cotton tee-shirt and a pair of torn shorts. He turns his eyes away from Anthea.

"Talk to me, Tyrone," she orders firmly.

His voice emerges as a breaking, high-pitched treble.

"Nothing to talk about," he says stubbornly. "I'm going to pay her back this time! I really am."

"How many meetings have I set up between you, your mama, and the social worker?" Anthea demands. "It would be better if you'd admit it when she's hitting you, Tyrone. She won't stop if you keep lying to protect her."

"I don't care what happens to her," Tyrone says. "But I don't wanna go to no foster home—and they might make me. Once before, they took me away from Grandma."

"Your grandmother has diabetes. Short stays are fine, but sometimes she's too sick to take care of you. That's why you got put in foster care two years ago. It doesn't mean you shouldn't tell the caseworker if your mother hits you."

She waits, but he says nothing.

"Or even think about doing—what you want to do."

"She's coming home tonight," Tyrone says miserably. "The hospital won't hold her any longer. In the morning she'll be back at my grandma's apartment acting like she's so happy to take me home to live with her again."

He twists the hem of his tee-shirt into a knot.

"Then in a day or two she'll go back to acting crazy. And chasing me around the kitchen and calling me trash. And telling me I'm no-good, like my dad." His voice is angry. "But my dad's okay, he ain't ever hurt me, or Astilbe. He does crack, though, and I know he shouldn't. I can't go live with him, either."

He continues in a taut, unhappy voice,

"I've got to stop her somehow, Mrs. Thea. Got to protect myself. Last time she thought I was Satan and she broke down my door. I made it out the window but she busted up my bedroom with a hammer."

"You're going to have to trust somebody sometime to get help with all of this," Anthea says softly. "But I know how you feel, Tyrone, I really do."

Her voice is low, as if she thinks out loud to herself.

"I wanted to kill my father when I was your age."

"You!" Tyrone is startled.

"Yeah, me. My father hit me around like your mother hits you. Even harder, though; he blacked my eye once. And nobody did anything, for a long time."

She wraps her arms around her knees.

"You know I was an addict and a drunk, don't you, Tyrone?"

He nods.

"I've told you kids about that, but I don't think I've ever told you why."

He is listening intently.

"My dad was one of the meanest SOBs who ever lived. He beat me up and he hit my brother Johnny. I was twelve, Tyrone, just a little older than you, when I made up my mind I was going to kill my father. You see, Johnny was only six; he had just started school and he came home earlier than me. I got back one afternoon and found my father, who was drunk and had lost his job again, holding Johnny's hand under the hot water faucet. My brother was scalded so bad he couldn't write with that hand for two weeks. My mother told the school it was an 'accident.' And then my Dad started yelling at Johnny, and worse than that, taking a belt to him. Almost every night."

"Why didn't you report him, like you want me to tell on my mama?" Tyrone asks.

"I guess, like you, I was afraid of what would happen if I told. Johnny and I were sent to a foster home only one time, but I hated it because the family that took me was really mean. No choice that time, though—my father had pushed my mother up against a wall and broken her arm."

She sighs.

"It was a lot harder to press charges in those days, and that was the only time my mother even tried. I was eight, and Johnny was two when that happened. When my mother and father got custody of us again I promised myself that the next time anything got that bad I'd handle the problem in my own way."

I am sitting on the step now, too, and Tyrone and I are both gazing wide-eyed, at Anthea.

"Did you—?" Tyrone asks.

"Kill my dad? No. Oh, not because I chickened out. I went so far as to get my hands on a small gun—a little twenty-two caliber pistol."

She scowls, and the scar on her face stands out fiercely.

"I would have used it. So help me I was ready to come home from school and use it. But I got a detention at school the afternoon I'd made up my mind to kill him. I'd figured he'd be passed out drunk in front of the TV and I could pull the trigger without him jumping up and attacking me. I kept telling myself I was acting in self-defense; that it was his life or mine, or my brother Johnny's. But then I was late to a class and wound up in detention for an extra hour after school."

She continues, deliberately.

"I sat in detention thinking about what I was planning to do, and how to do it. Whether I'd creep up behind the sofa or try to shoot from the safety of my bedroom.

And what would happen if I only wounded him? I knew I'd never have the courage for a second shot."

She glances at Tyrone, to make sure he's listening. She commands both his and my attention.

"But then as I sat there after school in the detention room a funny thing happened. Tyrone, do you know what I asked myself?"

He shakes his head.

"I started thinking, not about my dad, but my little brother. And I started to worry. Because I loved my little brother as much as you love Astilbe. And I had always taken care of Johnny when my parents were away from home, or drinking. When I was six I knew how to heat up his bottle and change his stinky diapers and get him dressed. I held his hand the first time he crossed the street, and I taught him how to swim and to ride a bike. I read stories to keep him quiet when my dad was rampaging around."

She sighs.

"I started to think what was going to happen to Johnny, if they put me in jail or a hospital, for murdering my dad. I knew I wouldn't get out for a long time. And my mother was an alcoholic, just like Dad. If she couldn't take care of Johnny he'd still wind up in a foster home, and I wouldn't be able to see him. I didn't think I could stand that, not being allowed to see him and not knowing what was happening in his life."

"I help Astilbe," Tyrone says.

"Yes, you do. And who will help her if you're not around? It's one thing to be angry with your mother, Tyrone. And your social worker and I need to help you deal with that. But you need to realize, like I did, that you can't stop your mother acting crazy all by yourself. If you did anything to her they'd send you away. Astilbe would have to grow up without you in her life. And murder is for keeps; you can't forget that. Kill somebody, it's forever, and you've crossed the line doing harm that you can't set right."

Tyrone is silent for a long moment. Then he says, "I run faster than my mama does. Maybe next time she gets mad, I can go to my grandma's. She can't hit me if I'm not around."

"That's a good idea, Tyrone," Anthea says. "When she starts acting a little strange, or if she stops taking her medication, get out of the apartment. Call your grandma or call me. If it's night you lock your bedroom door, go out the window like you've done before, and use the pay phone on the corner to call me."

He looks away for a moment, and then nods.

"Now," Anthea says, "I think you'd better give me what you've been sitting on all this time."

For the first time he looks uneasily at me.

"She's a friend, and she won't tell if you leave it with me," Anthea says.

Tyrone nods, wordlessly. He wipes his sweaty face with a damp hand. Then he moves, slides over on the step so quickly that I almost miss the exchange of a camouflaged object between him and Thea.

But I see the long, sharp knife disappearing into the folds of her sweats.

"See you," Tyrone says, and then runs.

"Today, I take it away from him," Thea sighs.

"Tomorrow, do I visit him in prison?'

"Wouldn't he be better off away from his mother?" I ask.

"Maybe. Or maybe not. The truth is that in his own way he still loves her. And he keeps hoping that someday she'll need to be loved."

She shrugs.

"They won't take him out of the home without proof that he's being abused. And he won't give it to them. I wasn't any different myself at his age."

"Was that all true, what you said about killing your father?"

"Wanting to, you mean. I didn't kill him—I told Tyrone the truth about that."

Her voice becomes bitter.

"I made the right choice that day in detention, and I gave the gun back to the person I'd bought it from the next day."

She stares off into the sky.

"But I didn't do my brother any favor when I decided to reprieve good old Dad. My father went on emotionally and physically abusing both of us, and we were always afraid when he was around. Johnny seemed to suffer more than I did, and even at a very young age he started getting into trouble with the law. I had my own problems as a teenager, getting hooked on alcohol and later on drugs. But Johnny joined a gang when he was eight and was in prison for assault at eighteen. I blame my dad for that, for teaching Johnny that violence was the only way not to lose. And I blame him for the fact that my brother wound up in prison. And that he pulled a knife on another prisoner who had a bigger knife, and when they attacked each other my brother died."

"I'm sorry," I tell her.

She turns, sadness in her eyes.

"Did I make the right decision? Would my brother have stayed out of prison if I'd done what I intended to do that day?"

She gets to her feet.

"I have to set an example for Tyrone. 'Honor your father and mother.' When what I'd like to say is, 'Vengeance is mine.' Or maybe I should tell him, to 'turn the other cheek,' and let his mother smack him on that side? And sometimes I wish that I hadn't been so high-principled and had blasted my dad forever out of our lives."

She adds quickly,

"Sorry! That's how much it hurts, even today."

She says goodbye and strolls off down the street, bearing Tyrone's weapon still hidden in the folds of her clothing.

In the Name of the Father

In the Name of the Father—
    "Be grateful to us."
Lord, have mercy. Christ, have mercy.
    "We are your parents. We gave you birth—"
On earth as it is in heaven.

And the belt comes down;
    "You should have listened—!"
Blow after blow;
    "You never listen—!"
As hands defend;
    "Say that you're sorry!"
Christ has died.

Christ is risen.
    "And you'll know better next time—"
Christ will come again.
    "Don't defy us again!"
Holy, holy, holy—

Amen. Amen.

To Beat a Tiger

"Are you feeling less 'lost' these days?" Father Joseph asks.

"Lost—?"

"Among the missing. And looking, not only for something that's been taken away from you, but for something you've never had."

I think for a moment.

It is noon on a hot Sunday in August; the service is over and the priest and I have lagged behind others leaving the church.

I'm sleepy from the damp and sticky heat, and I struggle to understand what he's asking me.

"I still miss Daniel. That part of me feels as if it's never going to heal. But you're right; even before the accident, even as a child I felt I was looking for something I couldn't find. I pestered my parents to death asking questions they couldn't answer."

"Questions without answers," Father Joseph says. "Answers that don't make sense. And a feeling of incompleteness in one's inner being. I've always imagined my childhood as an unfinished symphony."

"I think I feel more 'uncertain' than 'incomplete.' I waste time second-guessing my own decisions. I want to be a good person, to make the world a better place to live. But morality pleads for commitment, which I can't always make."

"Who can?" Father Joseph asks. "It's so easy to do evil and such hard, hard work to do good. And if any sin exists, it isn't in admitting you can be wrong, but by refusing to acknowledge you aren't perfect."

"I don't believe," he adds, "that we gain back a sense of self and move closer to God by strait-jacketing our conscience with iron-clad rules. I think compassion and trust have to temper those rules."

"Isn't it wishful thinking to put your faith in questions instead of answers?"

He smiles.

"Jesus said, 'If someone loses his life, he will find it.' And I know I'm not seeking out certainty here at St. Jude's. If people learn to trust each other, even a little, it means they're healing. But for some of them, opening to others takes as much courage as Jesus had on the cross."

"What you're saying reminds me of an Asian proverb. 'To beat a tiger, one needs a brother's help.'"

"Yes. Or the help of a concerned community. To face the tigers we're so afraid of and drive them away."

Vigil

Looking for God
In the pews, in the aisles—
In all the secret places . . .
Scars, dreams, memories
are etched as if a Testament on wood
And scored upon the crinkled, bobbing faces.
Yet once again, wonder—
Wonder . . .
That flickering
like candles left to burn too long alone
with each prayed syllable, something
Something changes . . .
As whispering worshipers name the Name
unknown
And opening their heart-haunted,
fear-riddled secret spaces
are named with the new name of Love
by One Who Is Known.

A Gentleman's Agreement

Something is going on between Sister Monica, Fred and Jerry.

Sister Monica is whistling a lot, always a sign that one of her projects is turning out well.

And Fred is scheduled to have cataract surgery in September.

None of us knows how she got him to agree to the operation.

But he and Jerry seem remarkably composed.

"Sister says she'll drive us to the hospital and back," Fred says. "I won't have to stay very long; we can go home in the afternoon. She'll sit in the waiting room and take care of Jerry; make sure he doesn't get scared. And she's thought of a way to help me with eye drops, too."

"How did you convince them?" I ask Tall Monica.

But she won't tell me, just smiles and says that it's a secret until September.

"I don't want to look like a fool if they change their minds," she says firmly.

A Litany Against Harm

Unifier:

Hear my prayer
I bring my petitions before You
And ask for wisdom.

From those who are silent,
I take back my language—
Renew that language.

From those without humor,
I take back my laughter—
Add joy to that laughter.

From those who un-name me,
I take back my name—
Let me grow with that name.

From those who abuse me,
I take back my courage—
Strengthen that courage.

From those who despise me,
I take back self-worth—
Deepen that worth.

From those who malign me,
I take back my truth—
Preserve that truth.

From those who criticize,
I take back confidence—
From those who diminish me,
I take back trust.

Nurture confidence and trust.

From those who misused it,
I take back yesterday—
From those who doubt it,
I take today.

Challenge the present,
and heal what has passed.

From those in darkness,
I take tomorrow—

Lighten the future.

And let me accept the full meaning
of Your love.
Creator and Preserver,

Hear my prayer.

Now and forever, Amen.

Keisha

Keisha plays for the Sunday service, the second weekend in August. Little Monica has returned from a week's vacation only that morning and slips into the back of the church in time to hear her star pupil playing the Bach prelude flawlessly.

"She's wonderful," I whisper.

"Too wonderful," Little Monica murmurs back. "She pays too high a price for being that good. I don't want her to burn out while she's still in her teens."

Three other members of the youth group are behind the altar this morning. Tyrone is the acolyte and Astilbe and Leo are assisting Father Joseph. At St. Jude's children don't have to fidget in the pews or go to another room for Sunday school while adults are in services. Older children, if they choose, can take an active part in the mass. Children too young to participate play in the aisle.

It was the youth group's idea to do this.

Even Leo, tall and uncoordinated, has never spilled a drop when he administers the chalice. And Astilbe, turning pages in the altar book for Father Joseph, does not wiggle or bounce up and down or chew her hair.

Keisha plays effortlessly as the service continues.

Father Joseph keeps his sermon short and to the point as he always does; creed and prayers follow, then a brief and noisy interval when people stand, greet each other, shake hands or embrace in a sharing of peace.

Keisha leaves the shelter of the organ and slips over to stand beside Little Monica at the edge of the aisle, while moving a few steps away from the people behind her.

"I'm glad you're back," the twelve-year-old whispers.

"I'm glad to see you too, honey. You're playing just great. But do you think you can do what we talked about? You know, like the Navajos."

Keisha hesitates, and then her expression becomes more resolute.

"I will," she says.

"Good for you!"

Little Monica hurries back to her pew, and Keisha returns to the organ. I take my place again by Little Monica.

"What was that all about?"

"Something I've been begging her to do."

The service proceeds; the twenty-five worshipers present go up to the altar and receive their communion. Keisha plays another hymn, goes to the altar and accepts her own bread and wine, then plays again.

After a final prayer, she begins the last hymn.

Beethoven's 'Hymn to Joy,' which, Little Monica whispers in my ear, Keisha learned to play in kindergarten.

"Do it now," the woman beside me intones, and pulls a large, pink Kleenex out of her purse and blows her nose.

"Do what?" I begin, but just then, on the last line of the hymn, Keisha misses a note.

Only one note, but the incongruity is jarring.

Father Joseph does the dismissal, and Keisha runs down the aisle, brushing past everyone else in the congregation, and throws herself into Little Monica's arms.

"I did it!" Keisha cries. "I really did it!"

"You sure did!" Little Monica hugs Keisha back, then holds her at arm's length.

"I thought you would be too scared, but you blew that note!"

"Because of the Navajos," Keisha says. Her eyes beam.

Her bewildered and anxious parents, who are still receiving praise for her performance, arrive at her side.

"It must have been nerves," Keisha's father, a wispy and emotional little man, accompanied by a smaller and even more perfectionist wife, says to us.

"She wouldn't have made that mistake otherwise. It won't happen again."

But Keisha, instead of looking chastised, as she usually does in the face of her parents' disappointment, only turns to Little Monica and, to my astonishment, winks at her.

"I won't forget the Navajos," she says.

Then she leaves with her family.

"What's all this about the Navajos?" I demand.

"I told her," Little Monica explains, "that when Navajo weavers make a rug, sometimes they leave a small space in the border. It's called the 'road of bad spirits.' It is placed there on purpose, as a mistake in a product which might otherwise be perfect, in order to remind the weaver that the design—not the rug itself—exists in the mind, and can never be finished."

She smiles.

"Keisha caught on right away. Her music lives in her mind and can be beautiful without being perfect. What I've been teaching her all these months of practicing together is the importance of letting herself make a mistake. Now she knows that she can and she won't worry so much about failure next time. And when she has to audition, or turn her music into a career, she'll be a better player for loosening up."

"I wasn't sure she'd go through with it, though," she adds. "She was really scared. All I can say is, bless those Navajos!"

Songbird (II)

There was once a songbird, caught in the coils of a giant snake, and the snake looked at its victim and said compassionately,

"Don't be afraid—it is only your time, the time which must come to all of us." And the songbird answered,

"I know that, and I am not afraid. But swallow my heart first, because that is where all my music lives, and where all the pain is. Everything else is just silence . . ."

But the snake knew that music is alive in the silence as well, and that the songbird underestimated itself. And the snake unloosed its coils so that the songbird could fly free, and music could flow forth from the silence also, and overflow the songbird's heart into the world.

Leo

Anthea worries about Denise and Leo.

"You've heard the saying, 'Men only want one thing?'" she tells me. "Well, that's what Denise wants."

"Leo seems happier, these days," I remark.

She nods.

"For the first time in his life he has a girlfriend."

She invites me to go with her when she picks up Leo on a Wednesday afternoon in late August. We treat him to a movie at a nearby mall. Charlie, his hearing-ear dog, goes with us, though it is doubtful whether he makes anything out of the creepy science fiction thriller which the rest of us enjoy.

Afterwards we linger at the burger palace in the mall, and Leo scarfs down three hamburgers, a chocolate milk shake and a double order of fries.

Anthea is candid with him about Denise.

"She's been pregnant once, Leo. I don't have to warn you about the birds and the bees, do I?"

Leo, still busy eating, only shrugs.

"Denise and I are just friends."

Anthea rolls her eyes.

"Be careful, Leo."

He swallows another french fry, and grins.

"I never thought she'd hang around with me."

He slurps his milk shake, and I remember what

others have told me about his background.

Leo's mother left him in a hospital emergency room, a few hours after birth. He was never adopted, because of his deafness and multiple learning disabilities. He has an IQ in the 'very superior' range, but has trouble matching his socks and taking out the garbage.

Leo discerned for himself, years ago, an elegant solution to life's problems, but it's one which puts him at odds with authority.

When he sees trouble approaching, Leo leaves.

He has run away from school, from the police, from six foster care homes. It is his way of avoiding confrontation.

He has tried to kill himself twice and sometimes loses his temper and screams and screams.

Rita and Tony, Leo's current foster parents, are pragmatic in coping with his inconsistencies. They asked him what he missed most, growing up without a family.

When told that he had never had a pet, they gave him Charlie.

The Labrador sleeps on the floor by his owner's bed, goes everywhere with him in the daytime, and Leo hasn't run away for months.

"Denise wishes she had a dog," he says, now. "But her stepmother's allergic to dog hair."

He looks at me.

"Did you ever see the movie, 'One Flew Over The Cuckoo's Nest'?"

I shake my head.

"It's about this guy locked in a nuthouse, and he isn't really crazy." He sighs. "I was in the Schuyler School for almost a year. Did you know that?"

Schuyler is a psychiatric facility for severely disturbed teens.

"I didn't know that, Leo."

"I didn't do anything bad. I mean, one kid had shot his mother, his little brother, and burned the house down. But I was the only kid there who didn't have to take meds."

"Leo had walked away from public school first day of seventh grade," Anthea says.

"Dillweed Jackson said he'd kill me if I took his desk."

Leo shovels more french fries, into his mouth.

"His desk?"

"The teacher wanted me to change desks with Dill. But he always sat closest to the door so he could get out first when the bell rang. He was a big kid, bigger than me, and really mean."

Leo scowls, remembering.

"The teacher says, 'Sit over there.' And I tell her I can't; Dill already has his books in that desk. But she won't listen. 'I want Dill over here,' she says."

He traces a catsup stain on the Formica table.

"Then Dill comes up behind me, and twists my elbow real hard, but the teacher can't see. 'Take that desk, I'm gonna kill you,' he says, and he's beaten up kids for a whole lot less than that."

"So you decided not to hang around?" I ask.

"What do you think?" he demands. "I turned around and started out the door. 'Where do you think you're going?' the teacher says. And I tell her that I'm dropping out of school."

"He told his foster parents he was dropping out, too," Anthea says. "But they reminded him he was only thirteen and couldn't legally quit school."

"So I threatened to kill myself," Leo says.

He looks at the table.

"I locked myself in my bedroom and pushed my dresser up against the door." He studies the table top. "Then my social worker shows up, and sits and talks to me through the locked door. 'Leo,' she says, 'I'm sorry, but you'll have to come with me.'" He laughs.

"I was out the bedroom window and off the roof, and halfway down the alley before my foster father busted down the door. There was a cop outside, though, and he grabbed me before I had time to get away."

Leo pauses a moment.

"They took me to a hospital to make sure I didn't get hurt when I jumped off the roof. Then the next day they took me to Schuyler."

"It wasn't too bad," he explains. "When I first got there I was really stupid; I thought they'd shock me or cut away part of my brain. I told them I was going to kill myself and they put me in a locked seclusion room first night there." He wads his empty milk shake cup into a ball.

"That room didn't have any furniture except a bed bolted to the floor. I didn't understand why they put me there, or why I'd been sent to Schulyer when I wasn't crazy. I was so scared that I cried all night long."

He pauses again.

"But that was the last time I cried the whole year I was there. I started looking out for myself, like the guy in 'Cuckoo's Nest.' I didn't like the food; it was lousy but everything else was okay. I read all the time; the classes they made me go to were really easy, and I didn't have to go to school with Dill."

"Did you tell your doctor, that Dill had threatened you?" I ask.

"I tried to but he didn't understand. He thought I should turn Dill in, or stand up to him. Now, that's crazy!"

He looks defiant.

"I mean, none of the teachers knew it, but Dill had a gun! I saw it in his locker. I don't know whether or not he ever used it, but I do know that he jumped a kid one night and kicked his teeth in. The kid never said who had done it or Dill would have killed him. And I wasn't getting my teeth kicked by someone like him!"

He mimics his psychiatrist's voice.

"Learn to defend yourself, Leo."

"Thanks, Doc, but I think I'd rather live."

He shakes his head.

"That doctor asked why I read so much science fiction. He thought it was weird. That I read it, I mean. He told me I should learn to play basketball."

Leo is angry.

"I'm in a nuthouse because I don't want to get killed and he's after me to play basketball."

"You didn't help your case by yelling, "Die, alien scum!' every time the doctor tried to talk to you," Anthea says.

"I wasn't going to say, 'Live long and prosper.' That shrink kept me in Schuyler for a whole year, while Dillweed was free."

He turns to me.

"Why do adults make kids put up with stuff they wouldn't put up with themselves? I don't think it's so crazy, not wanting to be around Dill." He sighs. "Maybe I'm just dumb."

"I don't know why adults do that, Leo," I tell him. "But I don't believe you're crazy or dumb."

"Denise isn't dumb, either," he says. "She wants to live on her own, because she's tired of her dad and her stepmother fighting. They make up, then fight the next day."

He looks at Anthea.

"We haven't fooled around, Mrs. Thea. Denise and I know about AIDS. We're just good friends, really, that's all."

"Then keep it that way, Leo," Anthea says. "Use your common sense and keep your pants zipped, because I don't think you're quite ready to be a father."

He grins, a quirky, lopsided, ingenuous grin, on what will one day be a handsome face.

"I'm okay," he says. "I like living with Rita and Tony, and I've got Charlie."

Hearing his name, the dog thumps his tail and whines.

Leo reaches under the table and feeds Charlie the rest of his french fries.

Long Distance

I'm walking down the street alone, and thinking
that in all the houses which I see
There might be someone waiting at a window
Waiting at a window, for me.

But I know it isn't true, it isn't true—
and maybe there is never going to be—
a door that is unlocked,
someone looking at the clock—
Someone waiting, and watching, for me.

Now I'm eating in a very nice restaurant
and the telephone rings, and along comes
the maitre d'—
And this time I'm convinced
there'll be someone on the line—
Someone calling, long distance, for me.

But I know it isn't so, it isn't so—
and maybe there is never going to be—
anyone on hold, who can't wait to be told—
The story that is locked inside me.

And a car pulls up to the corner
and I hope someone will say,
"Let's take a ride—"
For the one thing I've been missing,
missing all my life—
Is someone to ask me inside.

But maybe there's a chance—
Yes, I hope there's still a chance—
Do you suppose that there will ever be,
A friend to know, a place to go—
Someone who cares about me?
Someone who will care about me.

Charlie

Leo's foster mother tells me that the hearing-ear organization which trained Charlie acquired him from the pound only a few hours before he would have been put to sleep.

I am sitting in Rita's kitchen, in a small, brown, one-story house on a dead-end street. Through the window I watch Leo playing tag with Charlie.

"The hearing-ear people were told that Charlie had been picked up on a vacant lot," Rita explains.

She pours us both coffee.

"He was only a puppy. And he was hanging around that neighborhood for a week or two waiting for the family that left him behind to come back again."

"Left behind, just like Leo."

She nods.

"It's one reason Leo's so crazy about him."

She stirs sugar into her coffee.

"Apparently, Charlie had belonged to a family who were living inside their car. They were squatting on that empty lot, and the cops and Children's Services were called out because neighbors saw three young kids raiding dumpsters for food."

She sighs.

"The family drove away before anyone checked on

them. The kids are young and may be out there somewhere—malnourished, homeless, possibly abused. Two adults and three children, living in a beaten-up old car."

"Sounds like Charlie is the one who's better off."

"I know," she says. "Ironic, isn't it? The dog is rescued and given a second chance while the family scrounges through dumpsters and then moves on. A stray dog's life. But Charlie has plenty to eat now, and a good home."

In Demand

So I'm running along the beach
this hot summer day
sand scooting out from beneath bare toes
and the world forgotten—
until God comes tagging behind me
as a big black dog.
Ears flying, tail wagging
saliva spraying wildly from a cold, wet chin.
And God says,
"What are you doing out here, alone on the beach?
 I thought you were saving the Rain Forest
 or teaching battered women to believe in themselves;
  finding a cure for schizophrenia
   or starting a soup kitchen.
 What
  happened?"
"Nothing," I say.
 "No money.
 No support.
  Not much interest from the people I was trying
   to help, either."

And I go on running. Running down the beach . . .
Until sunset
when the air is a little cooler
and the sky lights up all pink and glowing
and God slips down out of the clouds as a snow-white gull.
And flying in circles around me as my feet hit the ground,
   God says,

"I wish, I really wish,
you would reconsider. I've missed you telling me
what to do, you know."
And God sounds sad.
"I know." (I'm sad, too.) "I've missed telling you, too."
But I don't change my mind.
"I'm not going back. No one wants to listen."

And I go on running. And God goes away. For awhile.
Till the crest of a wave wets my toes. And God says,
"They need you. I need you. So I'm asking you,
Think."
And I think, and I sigh, and then
regretfully shake my head.
"I'm tired.
I've given up.
I feel bad.
I feel—mad."
"I understand," God says.
And goes away again.

Not for long, though.
When the full moon rises,
and stars begin to appear—
When darkness has hidden the water
and swallowed the beach—
God returns in a whisper of wind.
A lingering, cool evening breeze—
and softly, so very softly
while I keep on running—
quietly, so very quietly,
God says, "Please—?"

Astilbe

Before services at St. Jude's the children decorate the altar. And on this cold and rainy Sunday in early September, Astilbe has brought in a vase filled with red and yellow maple leaves. Raindrops spatter off the brittle and wrinkled tops as she set the vase on the altar next to the cross.

She sits in the pew ahead of me waiting until it is time for her, along with Tyrone, to carry bread and wine to the altar for Holy Communion.

Leo is lector this morning. He reads a lesson which tells us that "every perfect gift is from above." But Astilbe's gifts help elevate this world.

She is named for a small flowering plant, and like that plant, keeps struggling to bloom. She is fidgety and impatient, never still, ideas and joy bursting out of her like steam from a teakettle.

She races everywhere, and would dart across the street disregarding the traffic if Tyrone didn't grab her shoulder to hold her back. He is her half-brother, protector, and best friend.

This morning she sings the hymns exuberantly and off-key, and doesn't so much carry the bread to the altar as dance it there . . .

I can tell by the way she stares into the distance during the closing prayer and recessional hymn that another great inspiration has overwhelmed her. When the service is finished she hurries to share her idea.

"You remember last Easter when the cat scratched me?" she asks.

"Yes," I tell her. "Your arm was a mess, wasn't it??"

And it was a mess, for the scratch became infected; a nasty oozing wound which ate layers of skin and needed antibiotics, multiple bandages, and several doctor's appointments before it healed.

"You couldn't go swimming till July," I remind her.

She nods, pleased that I haven't forgotten how much she went through.

"I've been thinking about Easter. Mrs. Thea says that at Easter Jesus died and came back again. Not like a ghost, but a real person."

"If you pinched him he'd say 'ouch!' like you and me."

"Yeah. And he had scars on his hands and feet like I do on my arm."

She shows me the top of her wrist, with its long puckered scar.

"I remember how much that hurt." I wait for her to continue with her train of thought.

"Maybe Jesus hurt so much—you know, when they put him on the cross—that's why he came back again. To help people feel better. Like the skin on my arm helped my cut heal."

"Hurry up, Astilbe!" Tyrone has been waiting for her. "Grandma's going to take us out for pizza!" Both children spend as much time as they can with their father's mother.

No adults have come to church with them this morning, and they run off together in the direction of their grandmother's apartment.

I think about Astilbe's analogy.

Jesus embracing the world like a layer of new skin?

I don't foresee that this is my last conversation with the little girl.

Neither Tyrone nor Astilbe show up at the youth group meeting the next day. They miss church on the following Sunday, though Astilbe is signed up to acolyte. When Tyrone finally appears again at a meeting the last Monday in September, he is silent and sullen, his eyes red where he's rubbed them to keep from crying.

I am visiting the group that Monday when he walks into the kitchen, alone.

"Where's Astilbe?" Denise asks.

"Gone." The syllable hangs in the air.

The group does not respond for a moment. Tyrone's shoulders sag. Then Sidney says, "Did your dad take her?"

He has had friends disappear during custody battles between warring parents.

"She went with her mother," Tyrone says. "Her mama broke up with a man, and she owes him money. Astilbe came by one night and says they're leaving that night because her mama's got to get out of town and they're gonna move to California; her mama has a sister there."

We are all stunned. There is no one in the group who has not liked and felt protective toward Astilbe.

"She ain't going to forget about you, Tyrone," Denise says. "Astilbe will send you her address soon as she can."

Pennies

Where do all the lost pennies go?
The ones that disappear
in the seams of jackets,
or underneath the bucket seats
of cars.

Where do all the lost pennies go?
The ones I have taken the trouble
to pick off the ground,
then spent to pay the tax
in checkout lines.

Where do all the lost pennies go?
Adults will add their fives and tens
and twenties
to the offering plate
at church on Sunday mornings.

Not their pennies, though—
you won't find pennies hidden
under one dollar bills.
Not unless a child who believes
it matters
has added a handful of damp and sticky
pennies
to the collection.

So where is it the lost pennies
go?
Children are the only ones
who know.

Sci-Fi Solution

Fred had cataract surgery on his left eye yesterday and all is well. If he has no other problems the right eye can be operated on in December. Fred should have most of his vision restored by Christmas time.

And now, sitting in Father Joseph's office, Sister Monica is confessing.

"You did what?" the priest asks.

"Alarm clocks," Sister Monica says. "I gave Fred and Jerry those UFO alarm clocks. Including the one you used to have on your desk."

"I wondered what happened to it," Father Joseph says. "Now, seriously, TM, what do those two old men want with a bunch of high-tech, infernally noisy and, to my mind, ugly, sci-fi alarms?"

"Once you set them you don't have to rewind them," she explains. "They'll go off at the same time every day, or you can set them to go off every hour. I thought if I took three of them over to Fred and Jerry's apartment, and set them for all the different times of day that Fred needs drops, Jerry would remember to help him put the eye drops in. They both liked the idea, and when I called them today Fred said it's working out like a charm."

She smiles.

"I think knowing they can still help themselves without having to ask other people to come in, makes a big difference. And Fred really likes those clocks. He says he wants to keep one, even when he doesn't need eye drops."

"Well, tell him to send mine back," Father Joseph says. "I was just getting used to it."

Stories

And God said:
"After two millennia, they've stopped listening. They need more topical stories."

And Jesus said:
"I'll try."
So he thought for a while, and he thought and he thought some more—

And then Jesus said:
"Maybe the Kingdom of God is like a little boy,
who has taken off his shoes.
and flung his socks over a fire hydrant—
and is paddling his feet in the water
flowing down the drain."

And God said:
"Water for those who long to swim in it.
That's good."

And Jesus said:
"Or, if you like, I could tell them that the Kingdom of God
resembles a teenager skateboarding down the sidewalk
while at the same time trying to hail a taxi."

And God said:
"Nothing is exactly as it seems. That's good, too."

And Jesus said:
"Perhaps I could also remind them that the Kingdom of God
is like a woman lining up all the tomatoes
on the supermarket shelf—
squeezing them to find the freshest,
and then deciding not to buy anything from that store,
but to go to the one next door."

God replied:
"Many are picked out, but few are chosen?
I think that you're proceeding, very well.
But, if you really want to hold their attention—"

Jesus said:
"What—?"

God sighed:
"Shouldn't you use a sports metaphor?"

Jesus nodded in agreement:
"Home run," Christ said.

A Tall and Barefoot Man

"He had such huge feet!" Sister Monica says. "By the looks of him he'd take a size nineteen shoe! If I'd had more time I'd have found a pair of shoes for him. But he was gone before I could get them . . ." She shakes her head. "Hawley's old boots might have fit, but they're split across the soles. I have to bring them in to be repaired."

"Don't blame yourself," Rita says.

We are talking to Rita in the grocery store where she works part-time. Rita immigrated to this country years ago, from a life made unlivable by fighting in two different nations in Central America. Now she helps one of her husband's elderly cousins manage this neighborhood store.

"You did what you could. You let him stay at St. Jude's last night."

"But he wouldn't go to a shelter," Sister Monica says. "And he refused to sleep inside the church. He insisted on staying in the courtyard."

"With a blanket, a pillow, and a jacket which you gave him," Rita says.

"But no shoes." Sister Monica will worry about the stranger, for a long time.

"He told me he's headed south for the winter. But he's walking. With only a few odds and ends in his knapsack and trash bags wrapped around his feet."

In September in this city the heat of the summer has dissipated, and it begins to be cold at night—a harbinger of winter.

I wonder, and know that Rita and Sister Monica are wondering, how it feels to have your feet separated from the street by only a few twists of black plastic; trash bags lined with newspapers and old rags.

"How long do you think he's been walking?" Rita asks.

"And what's going to happen to him?" Sister Monica is still sad that she could not find the man a pair of shoes.

"He told me he spent last Sunday night in an all-night laundromat, and the night before that camping out under a bridge," the nun says. "He takes the plastic liners out of garbage cans in public restrooms and wraps them around his feet before he starts out in the morning."

She looks at us.

"I never asked him his name. I wish I'd tried to find out more about him."

"He's a tall and barefoot man," Rita says. "Someone without any shoes, someone you cared about and still do."

Old Man

Old man
asleep on a dirty park bench—
this September day,
assaulted by pigeons.

Old man who snores
a whiskey-rumble thunder . . .
hole in one shoe
torn jeans with the fly winking open . . .
a nicotine stubble.

Old man.
A derelict whose slumber
disturbs my composure
even as others rush by, and I join them . . .
A stranger whose name
is unknown as I hurry uptown. Too busy . . .
Wiping the smile off my face I brush past him . . .

Old man.

Footsteps

Once I was a baby
chasing waves along the beach—
Sand between my toes
Heaven still within my reach—

And I don't know, don't know
how I came to stub my toe—
There's a stone inside my pocket,
It weighs so—
It weighs so.

Then I grew a little older
kicked a pebble with my shoe—
Tore a hole in Mama's apron
and she didn't know what to do—

And I don't know, don't know
why I chose to stub my toe—
There's a stone inside my fingers,
aimed to throw—
aimed to throw.

Older still, and with my boots on
grinding out a cigarette butt—
Don't dare reach for love and friendship
when I know how hate can cut—

And I don't know, don't know
why I go on stubbing my toe—
There's a stone breaking my spirit,
Hurts so—
Hurts so.

Now I'm here in a laundromat
garbage bags around my feet—
Lost my shoes a good while back
Don't have anything to eat—

And I don't know, don't know
how to heal a broken toe—
Dug my own grave deep, I guess,
Down low—
Down low.

Rita

When she left South America for the last time, Rita carried among her few possessions a deck of playing cards and a bar of sandalwood soap.

"The cards, because they gave me something to do, sitting in offices while people talked in two different languages about my paperwork," she says. "I learned to enjoy playing solitaire. Even though I would rather have played cards with my husband and son." She shrugs. "The soap was to remember my old life. When everything smelled new and felt young."

She is not yet fifty, this woman who talks to me in the lull between two long morning meetings at St. Jude's. But she saw her first husband gunned down on the street in her village in the country where they were born, grew up, married. She moved to another village, another country, and lost her nine-year-old son in cross-fire between soldiers.

She was a writer in her homeland, a teacher in the country she moved to after her husband's death, and here in the United States she has married a second time and co-manages a small family grocery.

She tells me today that she and husband Tony are hoping to adopt Leo.

"He likes us, and we're crazy about him," she says. "Leo has so much to offer, if he's given the chance."

Rita and I have never spent much time talking about the past. We run from the burden of too long-accumulated, painful memories. In my case, a stone and the smashed body work of a station wagon; in hers, shouts, screams, the impact of bullets tearing through flesh and bone.

Somehow, though, while waiting for our eleven a.m. meeting to begin, we do start talking about the past and its aftermath.

"You're beginning to forget, aren't you?" Rita says.

"Yes. And feeling guilty."

"I still feel guilty. Especially when, in my mind's eye, I can't remember what my husband and son looked like. For years I kept their pictures where I could see them, and then I'd feel bad because I didn't want to see them."

"I look at Daniel's picture and start crying all over again."

"I know. I didn't think I could make it, especially after I lost my little boy. But now there's Tony and Leo . . ."

"Whom you never expected to find."

"Who never thought they'd find *me*. They're survivors, too, and the best thing I ever did was admit how much they need me, and how much, as a human being, I need them."

"My life's been on hold for so long," I tell her, "I didn't realize how much it would hurt, to get going again."

"Like moving your leg after it's gone to sleep," Rita agrees. "The hardest part is to *make* yourself start walking."

Sanctuary

She arrives in time for service—
a woman
no one knows.
She has no friends
She has no family
She is an illegal
alien.
But someone has directed her to church—
some kind hearted stranger
or social worker.
She speaks little English, appears confused,
and nobody knows
not yet—
that she has seen Terror.
(The bodies of husband and son
riddled with bullets
in the roadway.) Of some South American country . . .
And so she understands suffering,
this woman who is afraid . . .
And she knows, she knows, about Jesus.
Her eyes peer past
the yawning double doors, and catching
the priest's curious nod
She crosses herself
rearranges her grip
on an old broken-handled straw bag
and enters the sanctuary.

Brothers

Yesterday six members of the youth group attended the Monday meeting at St. Jude's.

Today, convened in grief and anger, there are only four.

Tyrone and Keisha, Leo and Denise are in the kitchen with Anthea, who has marshaled them together in a crisis session. Kenneth is in jail.

And Sidney—sweet, impossible con-artist Sidney, whose one adventure in life was making money—Sidney is dead.

Before eight this morning, when both should have been on their way to school, Kenneth pulled a thirty-eight caliber pistol from his jacket and shot his brother to death on the sidewalk in front of St. Jude's.

Father Joseph heard the shot and in bathrobe and pajamas arrived on the scene in time to cradle Sidney's head in his arms.

It snowed yesterday, the first light, gentle snow of early October. It is snowing again today.

"I held him in my arms, and I baptized him with snow," Father Joseph says. He has been with the police most of the day, and is exhausted and distraught.

I stand with the priest and Sister Monica, in the courtyard next to a statue of Mary and Jesus. Mary cradles the infant Christ in protective arms, but the baby, victim of vandals in past years, waves a fist with the thumb and forefinger missing.

Father Joseph's shoulders droop; he is haggard and unshaved. He does his best to comfort Sister Monica, whose eyes are red-rimmed from crying.

"The boys never liked each other," the priest tells me. "We all knew that. They were at each other's throats all the time. But I'd hoped we were beginning to get through to them."

"There was an argument over something silly," he continues. "Kenneth says about the cost of a jacket. He lost his temper, pulled the gun out and threatened Sid. Then—" His voice breaks. "Sid yelled at him, called him a four-letter word, and Kenneth shot him."

"I don't believe he meant to," Sister Monica says. "He was showing off, like always. Trying to prove how 'cool' he is, with a gun."

"He didn't run," Father Joseph says. "He was sitting on the ground, rocking back and forth when I got there. Shock, I guess—I took the gun away. I held Sidney's head. He opened his eyes for a minute and I could see there was no time. I baptized him with snow."

He cannot go on for a moment; he stares at the ground.

"This is going to push Kenneth right over the edge," Sister Monica says. "To kill his brother! I know, of course, he's been arrested before. But nothing like this. I remember when they started coming here, three years ago; I didn't think Kenneth and Sidney were bad kids. But their dad kept going in and out of prison, and I saw Kenneth following in his footsteps."

Father Joseph puts a hand on her shoulder.

"I'm going to see him this evening. And Anthea is going to the jail this afternoon. Do you want to ride over to visit him with one of us?"

"In the morning," she says. "I'll see him first thing in the morning, but I think I should spend this evening at the convent. To pray with the other sisters of my order."

"Will you come with me to see the boys' mother, though?" Father Joseph asks. "I've promised to stop by their apartment this afternoon. Her husband's taken off; he's afraid of being questioned by the cops."

Sister Monica says that she'll go.

"You know," she says, "I think the only thing those boys had in common was liking junk food. I used to tease them about it. Offer them ice-cream or chocolate and you made a friend for life." She wipes her eyes. "Sidney told me he was going to make enough money to buy a Haagen-Dazs store someday. He loved ice-cream." She shrugs, perhaps afraid she'll sound too sentimental.

Anthea emerges from the basement with the four children.

Leo and Denise turn to walk each other home. Tyrone follows Keisha. Since Astilbe's disappearance the two younger children have become friends and turn to each other for support whenever the youth group gets together.

All four leave the church slowly, not rocketing off down the street as they usually do.

Anthea crosses over and joins us, next to the statue.

"They wanted me to tell them why it happened," she says tiredly. "Why?"

She scowls, her eyes tearless and scarred face twisted with rage. Her left hand is swollen; she has wrapped it in a bandage. Later I learn that she slammed a wall, hard, when Father Joseph broke the news to her this morning.

"I can't give them a reason," she says. "Anymore than I can keep them off the street. I try to offer them some hope, that in spite of the hell they've been through, life can get better. But the guns and drugs take all the hope away."

The snow is still drifting down, a gathering burden on the statue. From within the locked embrace of his mother's arms, baby Jesus peers out forlornly; his marble face cold; his unsevered fingers etching question marks into the lowering, midwestern sky.

Four Haiku

battered child
. . . kicking the swing
                higher

foster child—
all his rage spent
        I tuck him in

street kid—
whistling off-key blues
his borrowed Reeboks

drive-by-shooting—priest
baptizing a child with snow . . .
shuts his eyes

Graveside Service

Most of St. Jude's congregation attends Sidney's funeral service, but only a few of us go to the cemetery afterward.

The coffin is a plain, pine box. Sidney's mother has very little money; we have passed the hat among the congregation to help defray funeral costs.

The public defender is trying to obtain the best deal he can for Kenneth, who is slated to be tried in adult court.

Leo is the only one of the children in the youth group who attends the graveside service. His foster parents are with him and, of course, Charlie, who as a hearing-ear dog is allowed in the cemetery.

I stand with Anthea, Sister Monica, Leo, and Charlie while Father Joseph tosses earth upon the coffin.

"Ashes to ashes . . ."

"Sid was okay, even if he made fun of me sometimes," Leo whispers.

I realize how tall he is growing in the perilous middle years of adolescence. He is very solemn and wears a striped grey necktie and a brand new, grey suit jacket over a pair of well worn, second-hand brown slacks.

"You know something, Mrs. Thea?" he says, as the service ends. "Rita and Tony are hoping they can adopt me. In a couple of months we'll go to court. And I'm not planning to run away again."

"I'm really glad, Leo," Anthea says.

We hear the sound of an airplane overhead, and glancing up see a light plane emerging from the middle of a long bank of clouds. The sun is setting and the plane is only a small, blurred dot in the sky, far beyond our reach.

"Look, Mrs. Thea!" Leo stares up at the sky. "Sidney's paid for a plane to go to heaven."

Clouds

Clouds are massed
against the evening sky—
as a light plane drifts
through a rift in the clouds
where land and sky divide.
A cold wind tugs at the wings
of the plane,
and as it attains new height—
a small bird circling above the trees
takes flight.
And I look up
and shade my eyes to stare—
into the gathering darkness, as if I too
could be up there—
floating along with the bird and the wind
and the plane, high in the sky—
instead of remaining, transfixed on the ground
watching clouds pass by.

Denise

What Anthea has been suspecting for some time is confirmed, Denise is pregnant again, but Leo isn't the father. According to Denise, responsibility for this pregnancy can be charged to Sidney.

She has sobbed out the whole sad story after arriving at Anthea's apartment in the middle of the night. Anthea describes the ensuing conversation a few days later.

Denise's father and stepmother have kicked her out because they are furious with her for "sleeping around" and becoming pregnant a second time after the trauma of the first pregnancy and miscarriage last spring.

"My stepmother says I wasn't smart enough to use the pills she got me, and she doesn't want me and my baby in her house," Denise cries, over an emergency cup of coffee in Anthea's kitchen at two in the morning.

"She should talk," Denise continues, bitterly. "All she cares about is trying to have her own baby with my dad."

She goes on, "Sid and I didn't get along that good. I didn't love him, like I did Dewaller. But I thought Sid would stick around to see the baby. I didn't know he was gonna get killed."

She cries even harder, using most of the contents of a large box of Kleenex which Anthea provides.

"Leo is the only friend I have, and he's gonna be mad," she sniffs. "I didn't tell him I was going out with Sidney."

"This baby really is Sidney's?" Anthea says she pressed Denise hard for the truth. "Not Leo's? Because, if Leo is the father, he could be sent back to Juvenile Hall."

Denise shakes her head. "It's Sid's baby. Leo and I never did anything together. He's nice; he's never hit on me. But I went behind his back, and he'll be jealous."

"And that seems to have been her objective, all along," Anthea tells me. "She wanted to make Leo jealous. I was wrong about her motives for playing up to him; apparently she likes him. But the only thing she knows is how to tease; she doesn't understand Leo at all; what his background has been or how he thinks. He's head over heels for that girl if she'll give him a chance."

She sighs. "It's two fifteen-year-olds we're talking about. So what do they know about what they want? But they've helped each other a little bit when adults couldn't help either one of them."

"Denise will spend some time in foster care till things get worked out with her family," Anthea says. "Leo's in the clear. And I suppose I should be scared to death for this baby, but the strange thing is—I'm guessing it may have a chance. Denise seems to want to be responsible for it. Sidney's death has shaken her pretty bad. So maybe there'll be something good coming out of it all."

"And all of St. Jude's is her family . . ." I leave the thought unfinished.

But Anthea's nod tells me that Denise and her baby are not going to be abandoned, but will have a community to help them, whatever happens.

Songbird (III)

There was once a songbird, caught in the coils of a giant snake, and the snake looked at its victim and said compassionately.

"Don't be afraid—it is only your time, the time which must come to all of us." And the songbird answered,

"I know that, and I am not afraid. But swallow my heart first, because that is where all my music lives, and where all the pain is. Everything else is just silence . . .

But the snake knew that music is alive in the silence as well, and that the songbird underestimated itself. And it grasped the songbird tighter in a hard, coiled grip, until the bird cried out. And then some quality of spirit which had only been important to the songbird, began to flow out of the bird and merge with the proud spirit of the snake. And the snake's compassion and courage entered the songbird, and the songbird's music entered the heart of the snake. So that as soon as the snake released its grip, the bird flew into the air, higher than it had been willing to fly before. And its song had courage in it, and filled the hearts of creatures all across the sunlit world, with strength and hope they had never possessed before. And when they heard the songbird's music, they rejoiced and went home believing they had entered a new world.

And the snake continued on its way; through the low, dark, lonely secret recesses of the earth; and in those barren places where no flowers bloomed, it would sing the songbird's songs. And every silent creature living hidden in darkness heard this new music, which had never been heard in the depths of the earth before. And the snake's songs had dreams in them, and filled the hearts of creatures in sunless places, with a wonder they had never conceived before. And when they heard the snake's music, they rejoiced and went home believing they had entered a new world.

Christmas Pageant

It is two days before Christmas.

I sit in the congregation and watch Keisha, Denise, Hawley, Tyrone, Leo and Charlie put on the nativity play.

Denise is a proud, gracious, and five months pregnant Mary. Her child, conceived in August, is due shortly before Easter next year.

Baby Jesus is represented by a doll, and Joseph by an attentive if somewhat awkward and unkempt Leo; his bathrobe is ripped and he has pasted on a grey woolen beard to cover the few, thin, adolescent whiskers on his chin. Charlie, who as always accompanies Leo, wears a sign on his collar indicating he is a sheep. He curls up in the large wooden manger (one of Sister Monica's flower boxes) until physically evicted by a furious Mary, who tips the manger over and then rights it again to resettle Jesus more comfortably.

Keisha is a shepherd and Hawley and Tyrone are the three wise men. (Tyrone has explained to the congregation beforehand that they don't need three wise men because Hawley is large enough to play two roles.)

Hawley, being shy, sits on the floor to the right of the cardboard and plywood shelter which the children have decorated to serve as a stable and placed before the altar. Sister Monica is waiting in the wings, in the old, disused choir stall, to call him when it's time to come forward and present his gift to the Christ child.

Christine stands behind the stable. She is part of the play also, as she holds up a large pinwheel which has been sprayed with glitter to represent the star of Bethlehem. She is so fascinated by its bright, spinning colors that she twirls it contentedly above her head where the congregation can see, and she herself never moves.

"Cute, aren't they?" Anthea asks.

"They've done a great job translating Luke into modern English," I respond.

Leo's words to the innkeeper have brought the house down.

"I know the sign says 'no vacancy,' but Mary's going to drop this baby on the doorstep if you don't let us in."

Tyrone is narrator and Angel of the Lord, as well as a wise man in tonight's performance. He explains that the wise men have decided to bring the child presents he can actually use later in life. These turn out to be, as one at a time he and Hawley make their way to the front of the manger, a wallet with cash in it ("It's their junk food money; they get it back afterwards," Anthea says), a very dirty pair of Air-Jordan sneakers, and an old Gameboy.

"We hope you like these gifts," Tyrone tells Mary and Joseph. "Take care of them for Jesus, till he's old enough to use them."

Hawley decides to sit down in the middle of the stable, thus obscuring the congregation's view of Mary, Joseph and baby Jesus. He pulls back the purple bathrobe which has been covering his blue jeans and long sleeved tee shirt, takes his harmonica out of a pocket and begins to play.

The sheep barks.

"Peace on earth, and have a good time everybody," Tyrone says.

The star of Bethlehem crashes onto the roof of the stable as Christine suddenly tires of the pinwheel and drops it in order to go and investigate the stained glass windows.

"I'd say this pageant was a success," Anthea nods.

I have been wondering why Tyrone seems so happy. Last year he and Astilbe were in the pageant together, with Tyrone being a shepherd and Astilbe the Angel of the Lord.

I know he has been resentful and depressed, for he and Astilbe have never been separated at Christmas before.

Now, though, with the pageant over he comes forward and shows me a Christmas card, which is simply a folded sheet of paper with a drawing and a scribbled message on it. It is from Long Beach, California.

"Astilbe sent me a Christmas card!" Tyrone says. "She's okay; she likes it in California. Her mama's got a new boyfriend, but Astilbe says he's nice, this time. She thinks her mama's going to marry him, and she won't mind having him for a step-dad. She says Merry Christmas; there isn't any snow in California. It doesn't get cold out there like it does here, and she goes to the beach all the time, even in December. She saw a starfish at the beach, and look, she drew it for me."

Astilbe has, indeed, drawn a starfish on the front of her Christmas card.

"It's beautiful, Tyrone," I say.

"Yeah, well, not that pretty—she's only eight; she don't draw that good. But she's okay, and she sent an address where I can write to her."

"Her phone number's on here too, Tyrone." Anthea has been looking at the letter.

"You come over to my place tomorrow with your grandma and I'll give you an early Christmas present. A phone call to Astilbe, just like I promised when she disappeared last September."

"Thanks!" Tyrone's eyes are shining.

"Merry Christmas," I add, looking meaningfully at Anthea.

"Yeah," she says. "It's going to be a good one. See how happy he is about making a phone call? Peace on earth, and have a good time, everybody."

Starfish

Can you draw
a starfish with your crayon
and make the world new?

Can you pour
the sea into a teacup
striped pink and blue?

Can you open
a window with a feather
and let the light shine through?

Can you
Can you?

Home

I have been away for a month and it is good to be back at St. Jude's again, even in the cold and snow of February.

"How was your trip?" Sister Monica asks.

I have been on the Outer Banks of North Carolina helping my elderly grandparents sell their home of fifty years and move to an apartment complex in Florida.

"Difficult," I tell her. "My grandparents both hated leaving. My father and mother live in Arizona and have health problems of their own; that's why my dad couldn't help his parents move. He's busy looking after my mother. So it all fell on me. And my grandfather kept yelling that he didn't understand why they had to leave. What did I mean, they couldn't take care of the house, anymore? When they're perfectly capable . . . I couldn't get through to him about the advantages of making this move. He kept losing his temper and yelling, and my grandmother chewed him out like she always does when he gets stubborn."

"Well, there's your answer," Sister Monica says. "As long as they're crabby they still care. If they stopped arguing with you and with each other there'd be something to worry about. As it is they'll probably settle down in the new place just fine."

And sure enough, in the next letter my grandmother

writes, she tells me she has joined an exercise class and my grandfather is working as a "greeter" at a department store in a nearby mall.

The impending sale of the old house seems to affect them less than it does my parents or me, as my father writes of his sorrow and I shed sentimental tears, remembering holidays and vacations spent at the beach. My grandmother says when a person gets older, sometimes it is easier rather than harder to let go and move on.

But I grieve still, remembering how lonely I felt after the moving van had left and I made my final inspection of empty rooms.

Where are the Green Bay Packers?

Where are the Green Bay Packers
when you need them?

The moving men are crating the TV—
Grandma Alice's furniture sits on the sidewalk
and Grandpa Charlie wanders through empty rooms.

"I can't believe we're really leaving here."
He looks at me
through the corner of one narrowed eye—
creates a space between us, and hurries away.
He's thinner since they excised all the cancer—
and not the man who taught me to ride a two-wheeler
or bounded me on shoulders of iron
fifty years ago.

I stand in an emptied out bedroom
and yank the yellowed cord of venetian blinds.
This room was wrecked in a hurricane in 1954—
It was my father's bedroom
and later, when I visited, became mine.
I write my name in dust on the windowsill—
just as I wrote it on Christmas cards, long ago.
Whatever happened to the books, games, building blocks
which they sent me
And what did they do with my thank-you notes
painfully scrawled?

It's going to rain—
Before the storm we should be on our way.
But where is Jesus when you really need him?
On the porch, or next to the "for sale" sign?

Grandmother finds me, her pocketbook under her elbow—
She's wearing her same old, "it's-going-to-be-all right" smile—
The smile she uses to soothe and understand
Grandfather, small children
death in the family, or God.
"Are we ready?" she asks, her voice kept soft, reassuring,
as if I were in my teens again
and recovering from pneumonia
or a date who never showed up
for my senior prom.
"Are we ready to leave?"
Her eyes measure the room, perhaps remembering
all the other times
she has come and gone.

She looks at me—
and then as if sharing a secret, my grandmother
reaches through silence between us
and gives me her hand.

Baptism

At Easter we baptize Denise's baby, a healthy, squalling, eight pound boy, born at Children's hospital two weeks earlier.

His name is Leon.

And Leo, dressed for the occasion in his first new suit, stands by Denise's side as Father Joseph reads the baptismal service.

Denise has asked Leo to be the baby's godfather.

Anthea is the godmother and Denise's father and stepmother are sponsors. She is living at home again and the family is doing its best to work things out. Denise's stepmother is, herself, three months pregnant. Which, as Anthea says, may lead to some interesting complications in that family's future.

Sister Monica holds a lighted candle in front of the baby, being careful to keep it away from the child's flailing hands. The service proceeds, and little Leon screams even louder as Father Joseph pours the water of baptism over him, wetting his forehead.

"I baptize you in the Name of the Father, and of the Son, and of the Holy Spirit."

It is a fine, warm, sunny Easter morning: the service has been well attended, and everyone (except possibly Leon) is pleased.

"Good times do come out of bad, don't they?" Anthea

says when the service ends and everyone crowds around to congratulate Denise and gawk at Leon.

"Look at Leo. He doesn't care at all that it's Sid's kid. He's as happy as can be, just standing here. If Denise has any sense she'll wait for Leo, till they're old enough. He'll always treat her good, and he ain't the man to ever walk off and leave them."

Little Monica has taken the hangings off the altar, and as I look in that direction, a stray beam of light through one of the stained glass windows, highlights the checkerboards carved on both ends of the altar.

"This is a strange church, isn't it? Imagine doing that, to the altar."

This is a new parishioner speaking; a woman I have never met before. I smile at her, not knowing quite what to say, but she is only making conversation, and drifts off in search of more communicative companions.

"She'll learn," Rita says in my ear. "Everyone thinks that the altar is strange when they first come here. She'll get used to it."

"She's right, it is strange," I reply. "It took me a long time, to get used to it."

"You were like that woman, two years ago," Rita says. "So serious, and locked inside yourself."

And I realize that it is almost two years, since I hopped off a crosstown bus at the wrong stop, and took shelter in St. Jude's.

I back up, away from the crowd, and stare at the people around me.

Fred and Jerry are here today; Fred, with his eyesight restored, sports a new pair of glasses. Jerry is having a good day; no tantrums, and he smiles and chats with everyone he meets.

Charlie lolls at Leo's side. Leo is holding the baby for Denise. Hawley is here; he approaches Leo timidly and touches little Leon's face with a hesitant finger. Caroline is here, talking to her friends while Christine holds her own conversation with Jesus on the Good Shepherd window. "Five four? Five four?"

Keisha and Tyrone, Rita and Tony, Sister Monica and Little Monica wish Denise well.

Father Joseph is talking to the woman who fled from me earlier on.

I step back into the aisle and find myself standing next to a red-faced Leo.

"The baby spit up on my suit," he tells me.

"I'll take him," I offer, laughing. I spread a handkerchief on my shoulder to make sure the same thing doesn't happen to me.

"Always use a burp cloth, Leo," Anthea tells him, wiping off the shoulder of his suit.

I lift Leon onto my shoulder. He is sleepy now, and whimpers, and he smells of fresh talcum powder and baby shampoo.

And I understand something as I hold him, which I ought to have perceived long ago.

This is Easter, and on the very first Easter Sunday some lost, frightened people found an empty grave, and its emptiness was not what they expected. And they only discovered it was empty after the stone which blocked its entrance had been rolled away.

Those lonely, frightened people reached out to others

equally distressed, and soon those "lost" men and women became a family.

This is Easter, and the people of this church are my family.

I hold Denise's baby and a stone rolls over in my heart, and slips away.

I hand baby Leon to his mother. And I think about all the people whom I've met since I started coming here. The ones I see at meetings and services, and the others, like Kenneth and Sidney and Astilbe, who can't be here this Easter. And I think about the ones I haven't met yet, the people who may, at any time, walk through the red front doors.

And I know that my story is included among all of theirs; the gifted and talented, "marginal" people who've somehow been led to a church where the altar is carved into checkerboard squares, and jigsaw puzzles are affixed between stained glass windows. A church where trust keeps the stone rolled away from an empty tomb, and where they, me, *all* of us, are writing a story in our hearts. A poem a day, writing it out as we live it . . . A poem called lost.

Reflections

My neighbor's wearing
baby-spit on her chin—
across the street she waves
her toddler off to play-group
and holds her newborn infant in her arms.
I spray Windex on the mirror above
my bathroom vanity,
and blot with towels the tired look
from her eyes.

We're inside the mirror together, my friend and I—
Although I don't have any children, I know how she feels.
Another human being, who shares my disheveled appearance,
odds and blobs approach to life
and egg-streaked layers of anxiety sticking to psyche.
I scrub and scrub at the mirror—
Her vulnerability's mine.
But I can't wipe away longing
with ammonia D.

There are others peeking out through the mirror—
a woman who rides the "up" elevator on Thursday mornings
and answers the phones for a company
two doors down from mine on the thirteenth floor.
I see her leapfrogging happily through her twenties—
this woman who never, not once, has inquired my name.
I don't ask hers, either—

She cracks her chewing gum without apology
while I fumble through my handbag for a Kleenex.
All my allergies are acting up again—
"Allergies acting up again?"
She comments on this every Thursday—
I wipe away tears.

There are faces I scarcely recognize inside the mirror—
the alternate selves whom I greet with a nod and a shrug,
The bag lady who thanked me for a dollar,
The woman who purchased a National Inquirer
at the grocery store where we waited and waited in line.
She was traveling to the town where she was born,
to greet a father she'd never met before—
I told her a long story about mine.

The mirror embraces us all—
friends, strangers
women whose images help me to recognize self
and those who are different—
Our hopes, our dreams, self images are all part
of God's own countenance.
You, I—the Holy Spirit is in the mirror, too—
recognizing and reaffirming
We are made new—
made new.

Some World

There is some world, somewhere
where people are not afraid—
and are judged from the inside out
instead of the other way 'round.
Perhaps our job is to try
to make our world more
like that one—
If we fail, at least we know we tried—
That's the only thing
that really matters.

The Blind Magician

The man sitting next to me on the crosstown bus, when I go home from St. Jude's on the second anniversary of the day I arrived there, is a blind magician.

The blindness I can deduce from his cane and dark glasses, his role as magician he informs me about, and takes great delight in sharing his love of illusion.

"You're coming from that church, aren't you, Lady?" he asks. "The church where people whom nobody else wants, go."

"St. Jude's," I agree. "But how did you know?"

"I pass this stop all the time. I've gotten out and walked past the church a few times, myself. I'm not in any hurry. I'm working up to the day I'll decide to go in and see if they can use a blind magician. Because if I go in, I'll need to know that my magic can be of some good to somebody there."

"I think they'd welcome you."

"Well, it's always good to be sure. I have to have the cooperation of an audience, or the magic I do is no good. I don't play clubs, for instance—I'm strictly small time. I play benefits and hospitals. The burn wards at Shriner's—places like that. And anywhere people need cheering up."

"So, maybe St. Jude's would work for you."

"I've been thinking that it might. Don't be surprised

if you see me there, some Sunday morning."

"What kind of tricks do you do? Sawing the lady in half, pulling rabbits out of a hat, that sort of thing?"

He laughs.

"No. Mostly, I make people part of my act. And *they* do the magic. I help people who are lonely find friendship and people who are bored find amusement. I turn people who feel old into children, and show grumpy people how, for an evening, to play the clown. I don't do 'stunts,' but I play the fiddle and make adults laugh while children pull chocolates and toffees out of my ears. I do a little mind-reading, mostly telling people that what they're afraid of won't necessarily happen, and the future can still turn out right. And then the hardest trick of all—I ask anyone who's been part of my little act to talk about their heart's desire. And I make them believe in the idea that it will come true."

"My husband died," I say, not knowing why I'm feeling free to admit this to this odd stranger. "You can't bring him back to life again, can you?"

"No. But haven't the living already triumphed over the dead, in your world?"

"Yes—I suppose so. Is this the kind of magic that you do? Making people feel happy and sad, at the same time?"

He smiles. "Now you're part of the act, and catching on fast. It takes longer for the people who see with their eyes, but you're a poet, and you catch on quicker than most."

"How do you know I'm a poet?"

"You use words in a way other people don't."

We sit silently for a moment. Then he says, "When you write about the people at St. Jude's, will you write about me? Even if I never enter?"

"What should I call you?" I ask. "You haven't yet told me your name."

"I'm Barry," he says. "Barry, the blind magician."

"I'm Meg," I tell him.

"Magicians have always had reverence for names," he says.

I write down his story that night, as he shared it with me. And I know that wherever he goes, though the world seems a hard place for magic, his gifts will be handed out freely for people to use.

With the Shades Closed

"Seeing
isn't believing,"
the blind magician says.
"Sit a while
in your room, with
all the shades closed. And,
wait for it to get dark. You'll
understand then—
Seeing isn't believing."
This is what
the blind magician says.

Poems